tell me a STORY

16 SERMONS *that bring the* BIBLE TO LIFE

REV. DR. HAROLD E. SALEM
OF *The Christian Worship Hour*

Dedicated to my wife Beulah and my mother Clara,
the two women who made me the man I am.

Contents

Foreword

THE WORD OF GOD PRESENTED BY A MAN OF GOD IS POWERFUL—even life-changing! Proof is found in the life and legacy of Rev. Dr. Harold E. Salem. His ministry has had a significant spiritual influence on my family and me even before I was born. Harold arrived at the hospital shortly following my birth, just after Christmas of 1950. He came to celebrate with my parents, Merle and Marvel Odle, his precious friends and colaborers at First Baptist Church in Belle Fourche, South Dakota. His spiritual impact on my family spans five generations, from my grandparents to my grandchildren. He has ministered to us and prayed with us through the highs and lows, along with the mundane moments of our human experience. It was my honor to know Dr. Salem's maternal grandfather (who lived more than a century), as well as his godly mother, his father, and other family members. It has also been God's sovereign blessing that I have pastored two churches where his daughters and their families were involved. I (and many others) have received faith in Christ and a call to pastoral ministry through Harold Salem's example and encouragement.

Just after World War II, Harold returned to his hometown in the ranch country of western South Dakota to pastor his home church. Since that time, he has served as a pastor to thousands of people in two specific local congregations in South Dakota (in Belle Fourche and Aberdeen), and in the world through *The Christian Worship Hour*, which broadcasts the gospel of Jesus Christ through nearly every technological media source available in the twenty-first century. This remarkable life story has

1

been told in a powerful documentary entitled "The Heart of a Shepherd" (which is available on DVD at Christian Worship Hour, P.O. Box 2002, Aberdeen, SD 57402 USA).

At this writing Dr. Salem is ninety-seven years old and still proclaiming God's Word to the ends of the earth.

In the pages of this volume you will find a collection of Pastor Salem's Bible story sermons. Each one is a unique, humorous, and life-giving presentation of God's eternal truth for each of us. Though this could be said of all of Dr. Salem's messages over the past seventy years, the biblical characters and scriptural principles in these pages have the power to bless and change you. You will be transported from the frenzied freeways of contemporary America back to the powdery pathways of ancient Israel to discover that human nature and experience remain virtually unchanged— as does the amazing grace of God. Not only do the people of the Old and New Testaments come alive, but more importantly, you will come to see a living Lord active in the lives of people very like you. This same Creator has always desired to live in loving relationship with his creatures and has provided the practical means to accomplish this through his written and incarnated Word. In this collection of sermons you will consistently find the good news that Jesus Christ was born, lived, died, rose, and is coming again so that we might know our heavenly Father in a personal way. Salvation by grace alone through faith alone is the constant theme of these messages and of Pastor Salem's preaching ministry.

I mentioned that there is power to change lives in the presentation of the Word of God and that Pastor Salem is a proof of this adage. But I also said "through a man of God." To clarify, this life-changing power is apparent not only in his verbal proclamation of the gospel, but just as impressively through his living out of the good news through his dedication, devotion, decisions, desires, and delights. I have never seen him falter in his faithful walk with Christ. It is a blessing not only to hear or read his sermons, but to observe his experience with Jesus through nearly a century. We who have benefited from his faithfulness to his life calling are the eternal fruit of his labors.

I pray that as you read these sermons, you will come to know and appreciate not just Rev. Dr. Harold E. Salem, but the Lord whom he loves and serves.

Rev. Larry W. Odle

Pastor, Regional Executive Minister, Interim Pastor

Adam and Eve:
Created, Deceived

Adam and Eve:
Created, Deceived

Genesis 3:1-7

WE BEGIN IN GENESIS—the very beginning, the first book in the Bible—and turning to chapter 3:

> ¹ Now the serpent was more subtil than any beast of the field which the Lord God had made. And he said unto the woman, Yea, hath God said, Ye shall not eat of every tree of the garden?
>
> ² And the woman said unto the serpent, We may eat of the fruit of the trees of the garden:
>
> ³ But of the fruit of the tree which is in the midst of the garden, God hath said, Ye shall not eat of it, neither shall ye touch it, lest ye die.
>
> ⁴ And the serpent said unto the woman, Ye shall not surely die:
>
> ⁵ For God doth know that in the day ye eat thereof, then your eyes shall be opened, and ye shall be as gods, knowing good and evil.
>
> ⁶ And when the woman saw that the tree was good for food, and that it was pleasant to the eyes, and a tree to be desired to make one wise, she took of the fruit thereof, and did eat, and gave also unto her husband with her; and he did eat.
>
> ⁷ And the eyes of them both were opened, and they knew that they were naked; and they sewed fig leaves together, and made themselves aprons.

Lord, use this message to encourage us, to draw us closer to yourself, and to strengthen us. We'll give you the thanks in Jesus' name, amen.

Let's look at the story of Adam and Eve, looking first at their creation. The story is given in Genesis 1:26-27:

> And God said, 'Let us make man in our image after our likeness and let them have dominion over the fish of the sea, over the fowl of the air, over the cattle and over all the earth and over ever creeping thing that creepeth upon the earth.' So God created man in his own image. In the image of God created he, him. Male and female created he them.

Then also in 2:7:

> And the Lord God formed man of the dust of the ground and breathed into his nostrils the breath of life and man became a living soul.

This all happened on the sixth day of creation. First, God created the animals. Then God created a human being from the dust of the ground and named him Adam. It's interesting to note that the name Adam means "taken out of the ground." So his body was taken from the ground—but not his life. His life came from the mouth of God, when God breathed into that lifeless form of clay he had just formed. He breathed into it, and it became alive. Adam's life came from God, because all life comes from God.

That's why abortion is such a horrible sin. God gave life, and only God can take it. When *we* take life, even if it's an unborn baby, we're taking something God created and gave. We have no right to do that, and there's great judgment coming for it. If you've had an abortion, go to Jesus and agree with him that it's a sin, and ask him to forgive you. He'll make you clean. But remember this: all life comes from God alone, and God alone is to take life.

We read next that God breathed into the man's nostrils the breath of life and man became a living soul. That's an interesting statement, because God is a spirit, and a spirit doesn't have lungs. The Holy Spirit doesn't have lungs. God the Father doesn't have lungs. It simply shows that the Scripture sometimes use human characteristics to show some of the divine work and attributes of God. So it speaks of the arms of God, which doesn't mean God has arms like we do. It means that God has the ability to take us and to carry us and to love us and hold us close to himself.

Of course, Jesus has all the human attributes, because he became flesh—Jesus, the second person of the Trinity. God the Father, God the Son, God the Holy Spirit—all spirit, but then God's Son, Jesus, came to this world, and he was born of a virgin, and he took upon himself flesh. So Jesus literally does have hands and feet and arms.

There are four things I want you to notice about God's creation of man.

First, we were created by *God*. The Lord God himself formed man of the dust of the ground. Our bodies are formed by the very hand of God. No wonder we are such a wonderful, marvelous creation as human beings! How could God form the brain? How can he make an eye that focuses and shows us colors? How can he give DNA to a tiny baby when the DNA in our body can't be seen by a naked eye, and yet God equips all babies with that. It's like the psalmist says: we're fearfully and wonderfully made.

For the evolutionist to stand up and say that the human brain or the human eye or human DNA just evolved—that's crazy. To suppose that it all came from a puddle of mud, or from some lonely cell looking for other cells, and somehow formed into something that grew into a human brain—that is so wild-eyed that you have to really have to suspend belief. It takes more faith to believe in evolution than it does to believe that God spoke and God breathed into man the breath of life.

There's one question evolutionists have never answered: How can you make something out of nothing? They can't answer that. In all their evolutionistic teachings, they always start with *something*—the tiny amoeba or a piece of seaweed or a monkey up a tree.

God starts with *nothing*. He calls it into existence. So in the beginning, God created the heavens and the earth. It came from the hand of God and from the mouth of God. He called it into existence.

All Christians know where they came from. The evolutionist doesn't. He's still guessing. So we're way ahead of the evolutionists; you ought to pray for the poor things. They don't know where they came from, and they don't know where they're going. But *we* know where we came from, and we know where we're going. We're going to heaven through Jesus Christ.

So the first thing we're observing in this passage is that we're introduced to the human race. The second thing we want to look at is that we're created to have dominion over the animals.

In Genesis 1:26, God said, "Let us make man in our image, after our likeness. Let them have dominion over the fish, the fowl, the cattle"—and so forth. This is on the sixth day. So we're told that humans and animals are not the same.

God created the animals, but he breathed life only into the human being. He never breathes life into the animals. They're on a lower level, though some animal activists put animals on the same level as humans, or even above humans. But God says that man has dominion over the animals, and they're subservient to him, and he never breathed anything into those animals. He just created them.

So there's no question that man is to rule over the earth. Both Adam and Eve ruled it all. By the way, the beasts as well as Adam and Eve were all vegetarians until the fall of man came. We're told in Genesis 1 how sin came, and then in Genesis 3 came the judgment, after which animals became carnivorous and began to feast upon one another. The original arrangement went out the window. But when Jesus comes again and he sets up his kingdom on earth, it's going to revert back to the way it first was, and the animals will no longer be carnivorous.

Isaiah talks about what's going to happen when Jesus sets up his kingdom on earth. In Isaiah 11:7, we read that the cow and the bear shall feed, and their young ones shall lie down together, and the lion shall eat straw like the ox. So we're going to come right back to where we were in the garden of Eden.

Our third thing to look at here is that only human beings can worship God. A dog can't worship God. Now, I'm probably going to get letters saying, "My dog worships God; I can tell, because he's got his head bowed." Well, maybe he's sick, or something like that. I don't know. But we're made so that only human beings can worship God. Animals can't do it. And when we put them in a place they don't deserve, we sin against them and against God.

We go on to read that we're created in God's image: "God created man in his own image, in the image of God created he him." Now what does this mean?

Well, there's only one human being of whom we can say that he's the image of the invisible God—and that is Jesus Christ. In Colossians 1:15, we're told that the Lord Jesus Christ is the image of the invisible God, and so if you want to know what the image of God is like, look to Jesus. He was the perfect image of God.

Now, what does it mean to be in the image of God? It doesn't mean we just have hands and feet and legs and so forth. The worst sinners on earth have those.

The image of God is not a physical attribute, but it has to do with our behavior—with how loving and caring and helping and believing and trusting and forgiving and kind and gentle and long-suffering and encouraging and peaceable we are, and thinking more of others than we do ourselves. That's what it means to be in the image of God.

And what did Jesus say? "He that hath seen me hath seen the Father." Jesus is the image of God. If you want to show the image of God, be like Jesus.

Remember what Paul said in 2 Corinthians 3:18: "But we all, with open face, beholding as in a glass the glory of the Lord, are changed in the same image from glory to glory, even as by the Spirit of the Lord." What Paul is saying is simply this: we're looking at the image of God in a mirror, and we're trying to be just like him, and our image doesn't reflect the fullness of Jesus Christ. But when we meet the Lord, the mirror will be put away, and we will be in the image of God. We'll be the perfect image of God.

That's why Jesus said, "Let your light so shine before men, that they may see your good works and glorify your Father in heaven." Let that image of Christ be seen in us, and that's what we strive for, imperfect as we are, and though we fail all the time. I fail all the time in some of my thoughts and actions. But we strive to be like Christ. We have that faith image of what God is like, in all his beauty and glory, and this reality will shine when we meet the Lord Jesus, and the veil is taken away, and we'll stand in the fullness of Christ. What a wonderful day that will be!

So we must be born again. Only by being born again can we become like the image of God and get that image back. That's why, if you haven't accepted the Lord, Jesus is passing by right now and you could ask him: "O God, I want to be like Jesus. I want to have that original image that we had in the book of Genesis, that Adam and Eve had—and I want to be born again." Just ask Christ to come in to take away your sins, and he'll do it in a second's time.

I got a letter recently from a man who wrote, "During the service, I prayed like you told us to pray, and I found peace and I found joy. I have my struggles, but I found Jesus." You need Jesus, and you can have that image of Christ. Angels are not made in the image of God. Animals are not made in the image of God. Only Adam and Eve and the descendants of those first parents are made in the image of God.

Put your faith in Jesus. Put your trust in Jesus and rely on him.

Let's look next at the sin of our first parents.

Our first parents came from the hand of God, and for a home they had a regular heaven—they had the garden of Eden, and they were innocent. That is, they had never sinned. They could walk with God and talk with God. Now, we can look upon God at any time, but in their sinless fashion, made from God, Adam and Eve could walk with God and talk with God. There was no sin or discord of any kind. And we read that Adam walked with God in the cool of the day.

Adam was given the delightful job of tending the garden. There were no weeds or thistles or thorns, because that curse hadn't been given yet. And so he cared for the animals and he cared for the garden. He didn't just sit around and watch TV all day. When we get to heaven, I think we're going to be busy, and to be able to go to work is the most wonderful thing in the world. If you are a shut-in, you can't get out, but you can serve Jesus in a lot of ways. You can pray. You can have a list of people you could pray for. "Well," you say, "my hand's paralyzed. I can't write." Well just place a little calendar in your mind, and you pray. Pray for the church. Pray for people who are suffering. Pray for people who have lost a loved one. You can pray. You can witness to people who visit you. You can work for God in that way.

Don't be cantankerous. Maybe you don't feel good. Maybe the person waiting on you doesn't feel good either, so smile and be happy, and let the love of Jesus shine in your life.

So God walked and talked with Adam and Eve, and he made one stipulation. He told them, "Here's a whole forest of trees. A whole vineyard. Eat to your heart's content. Eat all you want. But there's one tree—" And yep, you know it; that one tree will be right where they're headed.

If you tell a kid, "Here are all your toys, but don't play with that one," and you go out of the room—you know where he'll go, in a beeline. Why does he do that? He's got that old nature. He maybe can't even talk yet, but he's got that nature.

And that's what Adam and Eve did. They went right to that tree, though God warned them plain as day. He said, "The day you eat thereof, you're going to die." And God isn't a politician who says one thing and never follows through. He tells it clear as a bell, straight as the day. And he's going to do what he says.

For instance, God says, "He that believeth on the Son hath everlasting life…" So when you believe on Jesus, you have everlasting life. Then God goes on and says, "and he that believeth not shall not see life, but the wrath of God abideth on him" (John 3:36).

Can you write it any plainer? If you will believe in the Lord Jesus Christ and receive Jesus, you're not condemned. If you don't receive Jesus Christ, you're condemned to hell forever and ever. How could anyone make it any plainer?

God told Adam and Eve, "Don't you touch that tree." There could be no misunderstanding. But that's where they headed. Who did they meet there? Lucifer. Satan. The old devil. The deceiver. The liar. The enemy of our soul. He was waiting at that tree; he knew they'd come. And then he made it so enticing.

I don't think it was like a slippery old serpent. I think that he came like an angel of light. Satan disguises himself as an angel of light (2 Corinthians 11:14). And so he spoke to them, and they were tempted.

What did they do? They took of that fruit, and the moment they ate of that fruit, they died, sure as the world. God was watching, and God saw them. And the moment they ate that fruit, they died spiritually, the moment they ate of that fruit, just like God said; then a few hundred years later, they died physically.

Now their innocence was gone, and their sinlessness was gone. They were sinners, as we now are. They saw that they were naked, and they hid themselves from God. They made fig leaves to hide their nakedness. I've seen fig leaves; they're just like rhubarb leaves, big and heavy. You can't see through a fig leaf. (God knows that today on TV, they could use some fig leaves.)

By making fig leaves to cover themselves, they were saying they knew they did something wrong, and they were trying to make up for it. These poor people! Then they go and hide. They once walked with God; now they hide from God.

I wonder, dear friend; are you hiding from God today? Are you squirming in your seat because you know that if God came for you tonight, your soul would not be ready? You know you've got sins and they've never been forgiven.

And what does God do? God says, "Adam, where art thou?" Calls him by his name.

He knows *your* name, dear friend. He knows where you are. You can hide, you can run, but you're going to meet God someday, and he's talking to you personally. He still does that. He calls your name.

He calls your name not to put you into hell, but to save your soul and to give you a purpose for living and a reason for living and joy in living. And so you need to respond, but you don't have to, because of the free will of man. You can choose or you can reject; you have that choice.

You remember when Jesus wept over the city of Jerusalem? He prayed and he wanted them to repent; he said to them, "Come to me," and he wanted them to come to him—but they would not. They exercised that free will. So you can just leave God if you want to. You can run, but you can't hide. Somewhere down the road, you're going to run into God just like Adam and Eve eventually had to face God again.

You're going to have to face God. It might be tomorrow. It might be today. Who knows? Only God. And so you have to put your faith in the Lord Jesus.

God pronounced judgment upon Adam and Eve. He pronounced judgment on Satan, and Satan is under that judgment, and he's going to be put in the place of fiery hell. That's what hell was made for—for the devil and his angels. It wasn't made for people. But if people will refuse Jesus Christ, and they stay with the devil, that's where you're going to be. You're going to be with the devil. I'm begging you to turn to the Lord.

So what happened with Adam and Eve? "For Adam also and for his wife, did the Lord make coats of skins and clothe them" (Genesis 3:21). God clothed them. How did he clothe them? With coats of skin. How did he get the coats of skin? He killed an animal, and the blood was shed. The blood is seen way back there in the Old Testament. In the first book of the Bible, we have this picture of the shedding of blood. Without the shedding of blood, there's no remission of sins. That animal shed that blood.

Now, that blood didn't take away sin. It just covered that sin. All through the Old Testament, they have all the sacrifices. But they only covered people's sins. And then you come to Calvary, where Jesus paid for all the sins of the past, and all the sins of that day, and all the sins in the future. Now as long as I live, my sins are all paid for ahead of time. So the blood of Jesus Christ is shed to pay for our sins, and if we confess our sins, he's faithful and just to forgive us our sins, and to cleanse us from all unrighteousness.

Hebrews 10:18 tells us that without the shedding of blood there could be no remission of sins, and 1 John 1:7 tells us that the blood of Jesus Christ cleanseth us from all sin, as black as they are.

So I'm begging you today to put your faith in Jesus Christ. When God asked, "Adam, have you eaten of the tree?" God knew that they'd eaten of the tree. But he wanted Adam to confess it. Listen, God knows you're a sinner, and he knows I'm a sinner, but he wants us to confess it. Admit it, and ask Jesus to forgive you.

Billy Graham says that when you confess your sins, if there's some big sin in your life—something that plagues you—name that sin as you confess. Name all the sins that come to your mind and that plague you. There are things you would do so differently if only you could, but you can't change the past. You can wash the past away, but you can't change it. That's what Adam did. He came to Christ, and Jesus Christ clothed him in righteousness.

God called to Adam and Eve, "Where art thou?" Today he's calling you. "Where are you?" Maybe he's coming to you right now. You could say, "Dear Lord Jesus, I'm a poor, lost sinner, and I ask you to come into my heart. Take away my sin, and I want to be clothed with your righteousness, dear Jesus, because I don't have any. And when I'm clothed in your righteousness, I'll be perfect in the sight of God, because I'm in Jesus."

I hope you will pray that.

Dear heavenly Father, we thank you for Adam and Eve, our first parents, who sinned in the garden. Dear God, in our own hearts, we know we wouldn't have done any better, and we don't blame them at all. Besides, dear Lord, you made a way of escape for us. You've paid for those sins, and none of us will go to hell because of the sin of Adam and Eve; it would be only because of our own sins, and because we rejected you. And so we thank you for this story in the garden of Eden. We thank you for so many lessons we can draw from it. We thank you for how you created man and breathed into him the breath of life, and for how you taught us to be obedient.

Lord, Adam and Eve didn't do anything that we would consider really terrible. They didn't watch any pornography, or anything like that. They just disobeyed you. They just broke one of your commandments, and dear God, I guess all of us have done that—every one of us. We thank you that we can come to you and find salvation, because you made it possible.

Noah:
Man of God in a World of Sin

2

Noah:
Man of God in a World of Sin

Genesis 6:5-10

⁵ And God saw that the wickedness of man was great in the earth, and that every imagination of the thoughts of his heart was only evil continually.

⁶ And it repented the Lord that he had made man on the earth, and it grieved him at his heart.

⁷ And the Lord said, I will destroy man whom I have created from the face of the earth; both man, and beast, and the creeping thing, and the fowls of the air; for it repenteth me that I have made them.

⁸ But Noah found grace in the eyes of the Lord.

⁹ These are the generations of Noah: Noah was a just man and perfect in his generations, and Noah walked with God.

¹⁰ And Noah begat three sons, Shem, Ham, and Japheth.

SOME TIME AGO, I RECEIVED AN ARTICLE TITLED, "If Noah Tried to Build the Ark Today." In this retold story set in our own day, the Lord speaks to Noah and says, "In one year, I'm going to make it rain and cover the whole earth with water until it's all destroyed, but I want you to save the righteous people and two of every kind of living thing on the earth. Therefore, I'm commanding you to build an ark."

In a flash of lightning, God delivered the specifications for an ark. Noah, fearful and trembling, took the plans and agreed to build it.

"Remember," said the Lord, "in one year, you must complete the ark, and then bring everyone aboard."

Exactly one year later, a fierce storm cloud covered the earth and all the seas of the earth went into a tumult. The Lord saw Noah sitting in his front yard, weeping. "Noah," he shouted, "Where is the ark?"

"Lord," he said, "please forgive me! I did my best, but there were big problems."

Then Noah explained. "First, I had to get a construction permit, and your plans didn't comply with city codes. I had to hire an engineering firm to redraw all the plans. Then I got into a fight with OSHA over whether the ark needed a fire sprinkling system and flotation devices. Then my neighbor objected, claiming I was violating zoning ordinances by building an ark in my front yard, so I had to get a variance from the city planning commission.

"I had problems getting enough wood for the ark because there was a ban on cutting trees to protect the spotted owl. I finally convinced the US Forest Service I needed the wood to save the owl. However, the Fish and Wildlife Service won't let me catch any owls, so I don't have any owls onboard.

"The carpenters formed a union and went on a strike. I had to negotiate a settlement with their union. Now I have sixteen carpenters on the ark, but I still don't have any owls. When I started rounding up the other animals, I got sued by an animal rights group; they objected to me taking only two of each kind aboard.

"Just when I got the suit dismissed, the EPA notified me I couldn't complete the ark without filing an environmental impact statement on your proposed flood. They didn't take very kindly to the idea that they have no jurisdiction over the conduct of the Creator of the universe. Then the Army Corps of Engineers demanded a map of the proposed new flood plain. I sent them a globe.

"Right now, I'm trying to resolve a complaint filed with the Equal Employment Opportunity Commission that I'm practicing discrimination by not taking godless, unbelieving people aboard. The IRS has seized all my assets, claiming I'm building the ark in preparation to flee the country to avoid paying taxes. I just got a notice from the state that I owe some kind of user tax, and I failed to register the ark as a recreational water craft. Finally, the ACLU got the courts to issue an injunction against further construction of the ark, saying that since God is flooding the earth, it's a religious event, and therefore it's unconstitutional." Noah wailed, "I really don't think I can finish the ark for another five or six years!"

The sky began to clear. The sun began to shine. The seas began to calm. A rainbow arched across the sky. Noah looked up hopefully. "You mean you're not going to destroy the earth, Lord?"

"No," said the Lord sadly. "The government already has."[1]

Well, I'm not sure about that story; there are some things that aren't exactly according to the Bible. But I can tell you this: you're going to discover, when you come to the Bible, that there was an ark, and there was a reason for it, and it's a great story. Because of Noah's obedience, he built an ark and he saved the human race from extinction. We owe a lot to Noah.

The writer of the book of Hebrews comments on this story in Hebrews 11:7: "By faith Noah, being warned of God of things not seen as yet, moved with fear, prepared an ark to the saving of his house." Noah never doubted God. Noah never disobeyed God. He just did what God told him to do.

God was saying to him, "I'm tired of this wicked civilization. All they ever think of is evil constantly. So I want you to build an ark, because I'm going to judge the world with a flood. I want you to build this ark, and I'll give you the specs."

Noah never doubted. Noah never questioned how he was going to float that ark or how to build it. He just started to work. God gave him the specs, and Noah got out his ax and started chopping down trees. He started building this monstrosity of a boat, which he worked on for a hundred years.

Now, that is fantastic, because Noah lived in Mesopotamia, between the Euphrates and the Tigris rivers, and approximately five hundred miles from the Mediterranean Sea. How was he going to get that boat to the Mediterranean Sea to make it float? They don't have roads or highways or anything of the sort, but Noah doesn't worry about that. He just gets to work.

After eighty or ninety years, he was wondering, "I wonder how this is going to float." Then he told himself, "No, God told me to do it, and I'm going to do it. I'm going to be obedient. It doesn't make sense to me; I don't see how it's going to work out. But God told me to do it, and by the grace of God, I will." That's exactly what he did. He went to work.

Do you know why Noah didn't doubt God? Because he was a mature believer. When we are mature in our faith, we don't ask God questions. Noah never questioned it for one moment, because what glorifies God is when he tells us something that doesn't make sense, and we do it. That's a mark of great faith. See how faithful Noah was! He just started, and he never quit.

We're so great at fits and starts. We start, and we stop; we're doing this, and we're doing that, but we don't get anything done. My mother taught me that if you start something, you finish it, even if you're not going to use it. That's what Noah is doing. He's gone eighty or ninety years, and he's still at it. After a hundred years, he was putting the pitch on the outside and on the inside, so the thing wouldn't go down, so it wouldn't leak. He's still working away, and that's what honors God.

Jesus talked about this. In John 8:31, he says, "If you continue in my word, then ye are my disciples indeed." Jesus is telling us to just stay with it, and whether we understand it or not, it's all right. But when God calls you to do something, you stay at your post even if it takes a hundred years or more. And that's what Noah did. He was obedient.

May God help all of us to finish strong and not to stop. If something doesn't look like it's working out, or it doesn't come the way we think it should or want it to, stay with it. Stay at your post until God takes you home.

Now, I want you to look at the size of the ark. That's given to us in Genesis 6:15: "And this is the fashion which thou shalt make it of. The length of the ark shall be three hundred cubits, the breadth of it fifty cubits, the height of it thirty cubits." That's God's blueprint to Noah. The ark was approximately 450 feet long, 75 feet wide, and 45 feet high—as high as a four-story building. The ark had three decks, and each deck would contain 95,000 square feet—about twenty standard basketball courts on one floor.

It wasn't some little rowboat Noah was building. It was huge. It would be in the class and the category of a seagoing ship that we have today, although as far as we can tell, it was like a giant raft, and shaped like a coffin, and covered with pitch inside and out.

Then God declares in Genesis 6:17, "Behold, I, even I, do bring a flood of waters upon the earth to destroy all flesh, wherein is the breath of life from under heaven, and every thing that is in the earth shall die." God is saying, "I'm going to send a flood."

Now, as far as we can tell in the Bible, there hadn't been a drop of rain up until this time. The Bible tells us that God watered the whole earth, including the garden of Eden, with a dew or a mist. For instance, in Genesis 2:5-6: "For the Lord had not caused it to rain upon the earth, and there was not a man to till the ground, but there went up a mist from the earth and watered the whole face of the earth." In God's creation, there were no deserts because this mist was everywhere. Everything was watered, and it was all blooming, and it was all beautiful.

Noah must have wondered: "How is this mist ever going to float this boat?" It's amazing, but he never doubted. We never read of him questioning God.

The Bible tells us that in the six-hundredth year of Noah's life, on the seventeenth day of the second month, all the fountains of the great deep were broken up, and the windows of heaven were opened, and rain fell upon the earth forty days and forty nights. All the earth was engulfed in water by this great and mighty God.

Now, notice this. This thing didn't happen overnight. God just didn't slip up on these people and send this terrible flood. For 120 years, he had this man preaching. For 120 years, he had him building that ark, and Noah was faithful, and God gave them time to repent.

I wonder when we're preaching, when we're singing, when we're having these services, and in every service we tell how to be saved; we give that sinner's prayer to pray to receive Jesus. And I wonder how many times people are thinking, "Oh, well, that's all right. I've got time. I'm okay now, and I'll put it off." Or they say, "I'll do it on my birthday," or "I'll accept the Lord the first of the month," or God only knows when. They put it off, and God waits, and he waits, and he waits. And all of a sudden, our time is going to end. You need to take that into consideration.

Here's Noah. He's faithful to God, though he got no results. Nobody was saved except his family. Nobody respected him. Nobody turned to him. Nobody came to embrace his faith and what he was preaching. But he was faithful.

Look at how ridiculous he would look. He stands there with this ark. It had no mast, no rudder, no sails, no steering. How would it work? How could it work? Oh, yes, and all these wild animals running all over the place, how was he going to get them into that ark? What a hopeless job, chasing down a couple of kangaroos, or trying to coax a couple of old skunks up the plank so you don't have a commotion there.

But Noah believed God. He didn't know how that thing was going to float, and he didn't know how he'd get the animals in, but that was God's problem. It wasn't Noah's problem. Noah's problem was to build the ark, and God's problem was to take care of it, send the flood, and put the animals in the ark.

When we serve the Lord, don't be fussing around and fuming and worrying. Just give your best to God.

When the time came, all these animals came, and there was plenty of room on the ark for all of them. It's calculated that there are about seven thousand species of animals in the world, so you'd have to have every species represented. The average size of an animal is about the size of a cat, so that gives plenty of room on that ark. There was no worry about having enough room on the ark. And there was no problem either in getting the animals in, because God spoke to those animals and they all came. He's the Creator. Noah didn't have to do a thing except get out of the way, and God put them in the ark.

Don't you wish God would do that with human beings, and say, "You're going to heaven—whether you like or not, you're going." But we are free moral agents, and God is not willing that any should perish, but that all should come to repentance. If you don't come, it's your decision. The ball is in your court.

Unlike with the animals, Noah and his family were brought onto the boat.

I've thought about those carpenters who worked with Noah for a hundred years, and yet they perished in the flood. I thought of some couples today—here's a wife who knows Jesus, and the husband doesn't, and they live together and they eat together and they sleep together and they go everywhere together, but she is a believer, and he isn't a believer. And when the end comes, he's lost.

Take a lesson from this. Right now you may be thinking, "I need to make that decision. I need to pray to receive Jesus." Well, just do it, and then you tell your wife. I always say that, because it's usually the man who comes last. I've been preaching almost seventy years and I've only known three cases where the husband came to Christ before the wife (only three that I know of; I'm sure there were others). The main point is the men usually hang behind, so don't do that. Don't be like those carpenters, and be lost and taken away.

Then we come to something sad, and that is, that Noah sinned. The great preacher of righteousness sinned. It says that he became drunk, and in his drunken tent, his sons had to come in, and back in with a cloth and cover him. This great man of God fell, and he fell in old age.

I pray to God all the time that I don't do something stupid like Noah in old age. I read of a young man who went to an old pastor and asked, "Pastor, how old do I have to be before I don't have to worry about sinning?" The old pastor said, "Well, I'd stop worrying about sinning about six days after I was dead."

We're all open to sin. Watch out that you don't fall.

Now what do we take from this lesson? What do we see?

First of all, we have to strive to be obedient. Just ask God what he wants you to do. and read your Bible, and pray, and God will help you to know; He'll show you the way. Once God lays something on your heart, we need to do it. We need to follow through, when we're convinced that's what God wants. And some of the things are so plain. God says that he wants all to come unto him in repentance, so you don't need to pray about that.

Be obedient to the heavenly call. Like Saint Paul said, "I was obedient to the heavenly call." You have a heavenly call, so be obedient, and accept Jesus, and live for Jesus.

Then we see as we go on that it's hard to live for God. It's not an easy thing to live for God. If you're looking for the easy way, forget it.

Living for the Lord is not sissy play, it's not childish play. Listen what Jesus said: "If any man will come after me, let him deny himself, take up his cross and follow me" (Matthew 16:24).

Dietrich Bonhoeffer was a great Lutheran pastor in Germany under Nazi rule. And he commented on this calling of ours from Jesus: "Jesus is saying come and die with me. I want your life, I want your will, I want everything you have. I don't want to be second. I don't want to be the copilot, I want to be the pilot." You and I need to put God first. It's the only sensible thing to do.

Noah didn't have an easy time following God. It was hard. People made fun of him. They laughed at him. You can imagine what they said. They probably told their kids, "Don't go near that guy. He's crazy. Something wrong with him. Don't play in his yard."

Harry Ironside was a great preacher, and a pastor at Moody Memorial Church in Chicago for years. Ironside used to tell about how he was just a little boy when he accepted Jesus; his mother helped him, and he prayed and accepted Jesus. His mother said, "Now Harry, you tell other boys what you did. Confess him." Sometime later, she asked him about this: "Harry, did you tell the boys you accepted Jesus?" He hung his head and said, "No, I didn't. If I do, they'll laugh at me." And his mother answered, "Harry, the boys can laugh you into hell, but they can't laugh you out of hell."

Just live for the Lord. People laughed at Noah and made fun of him, and they may do the same to you. So make a stand for the Lord. I know it isn't easy; it's hard. When I told other students in my junior class that I was going to be a pastor, they made fun of me. Well it didn't kill me; at least it hasn't yet. You won't die, and you'll just get stronger, and you'll shine brighter.

And don't forget that there's an end to the patience and mercy of God. If the flood doesn't tell us anything else, it tells us that there's an end to the patience of God. He gave those people 120 years worth of Noah pounding the hammer day after day. Those hammer blows were calling for their attention, like a church bell ringing.

God gave them 120 years, but those people thought, "Oh, the preacher down there! If I want to come to the Lord, I'll come after I've had my good times." I've had people tell me, "I've got to do some living first. When I've lived it up, then I'll come to Jesus." Well, maybe you will and maybe you won't. Chances are, you won't. You won't get a chance.

In Noah's time, there was one door in that ark, and one day God said, "Noah, get in the ark." Noah got in the ark, and God closed that one door. Noah didn't close the door; God closed the door. There was no repentance after that, and there was no mercy after that. There was only the fearful drowning of the multitudes. *You have your time.*

The Proverbs tell us that he that often is reproved and hardeneth his neck will suddenly be destroyed, and that without remedy.

The end will come upon you, because there's an end to the mercy of God. Don't ever forget that, dear friend. I wonder how many times you've listened to a service in your church, or you read in the Bible, and God was telling you to come to him and confess your sins and become a part of his body, a part of the invisible church, the beautiful church that will someday be without spot or wrinkle—and you turned him down. Maybe you're turning the Holy Spirit down right now. But you ought to come to Jesus.

Then the last thing I want to point out is that there's a rainbow in every sky.

After the flood waters were abated, and the vegetation was growing in leaps and bounds, and the animals were all off the ark multiplying and having a great time in this new paradise they had—Noah got out of the ark, and what's the first thing he did? He built an altar, and he dedicated all of creation to God: "It's all yours." That's what he did.

God was pleased with Noah's sacrifice, and he said, "Noah, this is a covenant that I'm going to make with you. I will never again judge the whole earth by a flood, and I'm going give you a sign as a token or a pledge of this covenant." And we read these words from God: "I do set my bow in the cloud and it shall be for a token of a covenant between me and the earth" (Genesis 9:16).

The sign and the seal of this new covenant—this new covenant of receiving Christ, the blood of Jesus Christ—that sign is that beautiful rainbow.

Clarence Macartney said, "The rainbow is the most beautiful thing in nature. How soft and mysterious and beautiful and sublime is that arch which builds across the sky, touching the earth as if it were to unite both earth and heaven."[2]

The only time you ever see a rainbow is after a storm. You'll never see it on a sunny day, when everything is bright and beautiful. On a cloudless, rainless day, you never find a rainbow. It's always after the storm.

That's life, dear friends; that's where you are. That's where I am today. It's after the storm that we see the beautiful things of life; we see the beauty of Jesus Christ. After the storm, after the adversity, after the trial, after the tears, after the heartache and heartbreak and hardship, then comes that beautiful experience. There's a rainbow in the clouds.

The storm isn't the end. When the sorrows overflow us, look for the blessing, look for the rainbow. The covenant God made with Noah was sealed with a rainbow. That covenant was coming in the Messiah, when he would pay for our sins, the sins of the world, with his own blood on the cross. That's the mark of that covenant.

I wonder today if you're secure, and if you're under that covenant. If you're not under that covenant, there's going to be the judgment of God. There's going to be the awful time, the floods of God's wrath will some day come and—not after 120 years, but in a blink of an eye.

When my wife, Beulah, died, it was just one breath, and she was gone. When God comes again, it's going to be just in a twinkling of an eye, and the door's shut. You'll never get in. You've got to have Jesus Christ.

I'm praying to God that you make that prayer, and say, "Dear Lord, just come into my heart and take away my sin. I love you, Lord."

Heavenly Father, we thank you for the story of Noah and how he saved the entire human race because he was faithful to you and was obedient to you. We pray today that we'll take lessons from Noah, and never doubt you, Lord, and always obey you to the best of our ability, and be listening for your Spirit, and to read in the Word of God what you want us to do and not to do. Thank you that you bless us and help us.

We thank you for the promises of your word, dear Lord, that you will always be with us, to help us through the hard times of life. I know some that are really having a tough go of it. It just seems like the devil is afflicting them. But out of their suffering and out of their struggles, they are a shining light for you. Help them to persevere, to lean on you, and hang on, and the day will come when the bright sun will shine again. Bless us, Lord, and draw us closer to yourself.

We pray in the Savior's name, amen.

Joseph:
From Rags to Riches

3

Joseph:
From Rags to Riches

Genesis 41:39-44

³⁹ And Pharaoh said unto Joseph, Forasmuch as God hath shewed thee all this, there is none so discreet and wise as thou art:

⁴⁰ Thou shalt be over my house, and according unto thy word shall all my people be ruled: only in the throne will I be greater than thou.

⁴¹ And Pharaoh said unto Joseph, See, I have set thee over all the land of Egypt.

⁴² And Pharaoh took off his ring from his hand, and put it upon Joseph's hand, and arrayed him in vestures of fine linen, and put a gold chain about his neck;

⁴³ And he made him to ride in the second chariot which he had; and they cried before him, Bow the knee: and he made him ruler over all the land of Egypt.

⁴⁴ And Pharaoh said unto Joseph, I am Pharaoh, and without thee shall no man lift up his hand or foot in all the land of Egypt.

WE SEE JESUS IN THIS MAN JOSEPH. Joseph is in Egypt, and he's enslaved, having been sold into slavery. He's put on the block, and Pharaoh has the captain of his guard come by, a man named Potiphar.

Potiphar needs a strong young man. So he'll come check the young men's health, and he'll see where they're from. He may even pinch them, feel their muscles.

Potiphar looks at Joseph, and he buys him.

Joseph eventually became a captain in Pharaoh's army. He came to be the second highest man in all of Egypt. And it came to pass because Pharaoh had a dream. He had a dream of seven cows coming up out of the Nile River. They were all fat and heavy cows. Then there came skinny cows, and they ate the fat cows. Cannibal cows, I guess; I don't know.

It was just a dream, and Pharaoh couldn't understand it. He asked his magicians if they could tell him what the dream meant. None of them could tell him. But then they remembered that Joseph, who was in prison, had helped the baker and helped the butler by telling them what their dreams meant.

So they brought Joseph out of prison. The first thing Joseph did when he stood before Pharaoh was to give praise to God. He gave God the credit before he ever said a word. Then he gave the interpretation of the dream: there was going to be a famine, but first there would be seven great years of prosperous, bountiful crops. Then would come seven years of famine.

Joseph said, "You need to have somebody in those first seven years to take charge and store food away and plan for the famine. When the famine comes, have the same man distribute the food, so you can get through those seven years of famine." It was a marvelous interpretation of the dream.

Pharaoh looked at Joseph and said, "With all your wisdom, you will be the man, and you're going to be second only to me. Only I will have more power in this kingdom. You're going to ride in a chariot just behind me. You're going to be one of the rulers of Egypt."

I entitled this message "From Rags to Riches." Here was Joseph, in this lousy prison. It wasn't like a nice motel. It was a dungeon, and it was a horrible place. He was taken out of that dungeon and elevated to be the second ruler of Egypt. From rags to riches.

The question comes right away: Can Joseph handle prosperity? Can he handle riches? Most people can't. It's a temptation. It's a trial. It's a fierce problem, and people have fallen into riches, and it's a ruination more times than not. It is easier to handle adversity than it is to handle prosperity.

When I was young, I thought that if I had a lot of money, I would be so happy. I would have everything at my beck and call.

I want to tell you something: God has a plan for your life. He has a blueprint for your life, a detailed plan. What you need to do is make him the Lord of your life. You do that by receiving him as your Savior, then making him your Lord so that you read his word and you follow him the best you can. He'll show you the way, and he'll use you. Don't let age hinder you from starting out walking with the Lord and serving the Lord.

In this story, Joseph was about thirty years old when all the riches of Egypt were heaped upon him—just at the time in life when it would be the most tempting.

The Bible is filled with young people who are so faithful to God. Look at David. He wasn't even twenty years old when Samuel came and anointed him to be the king of all Israel. He was only thirty years old when be became king; he had to wait ten years after he was anointed by Samuel.

Samuel, when he was thirty years old, ruled all of Israel, and he did it well.

When Daniel was picked by Nebuchadnezzar to be one of his chosen men in battle, he was only a boy.

Then there was Josiah, eight years old when he began to reign in Israel, and he did a great job of it.

Mary, the mother of our Lord, most probably was a teenager when she gave birth to the Lord Jesus Christ.

Don't say that you have to be an older person before you can serve Jesus. The Lord is looking for young people who have all their lives before them, like Joseph. If you dedicate your life to him, you can walk with the Lord and be used of the Lord.

Charles Haddon Spurgeon, who is called the Prince of Preachers, took the pulpit in London's New Park Street Chapel when he was twenty years old. He filled the place to capacity when he was thirty years old.

Then there's G. Campbell Morgan, the Prince of Expositors. He was thirteen years old when he preached his first sermon. When he was thirty-three, he was called the Bible Teacher of England.

Like Joseph, we have to be open to the Lord. Like Joseph, we have to be careful of prosperity. Clarence Macartney puts it this way: "Joseph is now to be tried by prosperity. That's a greater trial than adversity. The man who has fallen heir to a fortune is in greater moral peril than the man who has lost one."

J. Oswald Sanders once said, "Not every man can carry a full cup. Sudden elevation frequently leads to pride and a fall. The most exacting test of all to survive is prosperity."[3]

How's Joseph going to do it? Well, let's take a look at this.

Sometimes, prosperity becomes deceiving. People think if they have their money, they have everything. They think that with money, whatever they need they can have—so the more money, the happier they'll be.

I used to think like that when I was a kid. I was a child of the Great Depression. We didn't have a nickel. I thought if I had $100, I'd be wealthy. We dreamed of all of those things; if we had money, we would be happy.

You remember the story of King Midas; it's a fairytale from ancient Greece. You probably know the story. And oh, does it have a good lesson for us! Midas was a very good and kind king, and everybody loved him. He was so kind that the god Dionysus came and said, "I'll give you one wish, Midas—whatever you wish for." Well, Midas wished that everything he touched would turn to gold. He would have gold, gold, gold. Dionysus said, "All right, your wish is granted."

Midas went out and he touched all the silver he had. All of it turned to gold. Then he saw a haystack, and he went and touched the haystack, and the whole haystack was filled with solid gold. He couldn't believe it. He was filled with happiness—until he forgot, and he picked a flower. The beautiful rose turned to cold gold. Then he grew hungry, but the food he touched turned to gold. You can love gold, and you can worship gold, but you can't eat gold.

There he was, starving. But the most terribly tragic thing happened next. His little daughter came running in, and when he put his arms around her, she became a cold statue of gold. Midas saw what a horrible thing had happened.

I have children, I have grandchildren, and I have great-grandchildren. For them to put their arms around you and give you a hug and a kiss— that's seventh heaven! Especially since my wife, Beulah, has been gone.

But here was this man Midas, broken-hearted. It was a curse.

He prayed for Dionysus to have sympathy on him and take back that wish. Dionysus agreed, and he took it back. Midas was suddenly as poor as a church mouse, but he became the happiest man on earth.

Let's get this thinking out of our minds that just having wealth will ever bring happiness. You can have a million-dollar house, but if it isn't a home, what good is it? You can have a million-dollar ring, but if there isn't any love with it, what good is it?

God told us pastors to shepherd the flock, and then, in Paul's words to Timothy, he tells us this:

> Command those who are rich in this present world not to be arrogant, nor to put their hope in wealth, which is so uncertain, but to put their hope in God, who richly provides us with everything for our enjoyment. Command them to do good, to be rich in good deeds, and to be generous and willing to share. In this way they will lay up treasure for themselves as a firm foundation for the coming age, so that they may take hold of the life that is truly life. (1 Timothy 6:17-19 NIV)

There's a famous Jewish story the rabbis tell. A man called Monoboz inherited great wealth. He was a good man, a kind and generous man. When a famine came, there were poor people everywhere, and Monoboz started giving all his money away to the starving.

His relatives came and complained about this. They said, "Your fathers laid up treasure, and they added to the treasure they inherited from their fathers. Are you just going to waste it all?"

Monoboz replied, "My fathers laid up treasures below; I've laid up treasures above. My fathers laid up treasures of mammon; I've laid up treasures of souls. My fathers laid up treasures for this world; I've laid up treasures for the world to come."

Warren Wiersbe said, "God did not condemn riches or rich people. He condemned the wrong use of riches, and rich people who use their wealth as a weapon, and not as a tool with which to build."[4]

David said, "If riches increase, set not your heart upon them" (Psalm 62:10).

We ask the question: Joseph is very rich; how's he going to handle it? Well, he wasn't deceived by riches. You know the story. He was surrounded by them, but he never took his eyes off his wonderful God. He didn't bow down to riches. Prosperity never fazed him, never touched him.

Sometimes when people get money, they forget God. I've seen that in my ministry. They've been poor as a church mouse, they've been faithful as they could be; then they fall into money, and they get a good car, and God only knows where they're running around to in that good car, living it up. Wealth was the worst thing that could ever happen to them. Their lifestyle changes drastically. They're no longer close to God or close to church.

No, Joseph never did that. He was rich, rich, rich. But he never forgot God.

Sometimes prosperity makes people proud. I've seen them strut all over the place like peacocks. Maybe they discover gold or oil on their land, and they're rich. Where I came from, they discovered bentonite. We had people out there who couldn't write their numbers to ten, then they discovered bentonite and they were rich, driving around in Cadillacs. Just as rich as they could be, and they thought they were pretty smart, pretty clever. Here they were; they had money, and others didn't. Then they would suggest, in a subtle way, "Well, if you were as smart and industrious as I am, then you'd have money like I have." It went to their head.

Let me tell you, friend, if you think you have all your money because you're so brilliant, let me give you what I call the brick test. The brick test is real easy. You just walk under the scaffolding of some bricklayer and let him drop a brick on your head. Then you see how smart you are as you lie there in the gutter, knocked out cold, hearing whistles and bells, with lights flickering, and trying to uncross your crossed eyes. You're lying there. See how smart you are then.

You see, if you have prospered materially, thank God for it. You've been entrusted with something by God. But you may have your money because you didn't pay your employees, or you cheated on your taxes, or you worked on somebody else's weakness—like buying lottery tickets. A Christian ought never to buy a lottery ticket, because all you're doing is trying to get something for nothing. You're taking something that some poor person, who's weaker than you are, has put his money into, and you're going to get it if you win the lottery. A Christian ought never to be caught dead with a lottery ticket.

What did this great man Joseph do? He was true, and he never failed. He didn't get proud.

Sometimes when people get money, they forget their friends. They'll have close relationships that are broken, and they'll take up with a new class of people. They'll get in the high society. They travel with a different crowd. They'll run around with a bunch of people who don't know God. I'm not saying that all high society doesn't know God, but a lot of them don't, at least in the culture I see. Sometimes they forget blood relatives. Hard to believe that people would turn against blood relatives if they have wealth and the relatives don't.

Joseph didn't do that. He was the prime minister of a powerful world empire, living in splendor, second only to the king. People bowed before him when he rode in that fancy beautiful chariot (it probably had gold overlaid on it). He was clothed in fine linen and he wore the king's signet ring. He had servants all over the place.

People might say, "I wonder if Joseph is going to forget God? He's living pretty high. He's got a lot of things. I wonder if he's going to forget God?"

Though Egypt had given him everything, Joseph never became Egyptianized. Egypt made him famous beyond description. As a matter of fact, he even married one of the priest's daughters. And Pharaoh gave him an Egyptian name: Zaphnath-Paaneah. They wanted to make him an Egyptian.

But when his sons were born, we get a little inkling of Joseph's different mindset. He named his firstborn Manasseh, which means "God has made me forget." Joseph said, "God hath made me forget all of my toil." That is, the troubles of the past were all taken away, and Joseph was a thankful man praising God.

When his second son was born, Joseph named him Ephraim, which means "be fruitful," and Joseph said, "God has caused me to be fruitful in the land of my affliction." He didn't forget his God.

Joseph had not forgotten his father, Jacob, but he had forgotten the hard things of life. He had forgotten his brothers' hatred against him. He forgot the angry eyes of his brothers and their gruff voices, and how they stripped him of his beautiful coat of many colors and ripped it to shreds. He forgot how they put him in a cistern infested with vermin. He forgot how they took him out of that cistern when the caravan came through, and how they threw him down before the slave traders and said, "Do with him as you wish. He's all yours." Joseph forgot all that. He's a big man. He's a great man. He's a godly man.

But Joseph hadn't forgotten his father, or Benjamin, the younger brother he so loved. With all his wealth and prestige and power and honor, he never forgot his family. He lived in Egypt, and Egypt was a beautiful place. They had great palaces along the Nile River. They had beautiful palm trees. They had the Great Sphinx, they had those colossal pyramids. They had all the glory of that land at that time.

Joseph saw all this, and the grand and glorious scenes just faded away. Instead, he started thinking. He was thinking about a little village over there in Hebron. He was thinking about the goat-hide tents of his brothers, and the white dots of the flocks of sheep on the hillsides around Dothan and around Hebron. He thought of those beautiful hills of Judea. He thought of the gnarled oaks of Mamre.

He thought of all those things, and Joseph said to himself, "Does my father still live, or does he sleep now in the cave of Machpelah by the side of Abraham and Isaac? My brother Benjamin—is he alive?"

Look at that! Here was Joseph, prime minister of Egypt, rich and powerful, second only to Pharaoh, prosperity all over the place. Will he forget his family? Never in a thousand years.

Clarence Macartney has a beautiful passage that I just have to share with you:

> I think that when all of the boys and their wives had their flocks out in the fields, and Jacob is alone in his tent, I think he probably went to an old black chest. He opened it up and he took out a garment. It was that bloody torn garment of Joseph. He would put it over his knees and he would think of Joseph. Then he would put it back, and then from that old chest he would take a scarlet silk scarf that Rachel used to wear in her hair. He would take that and he would kiss it. And the tears would flow. It would flow just like the day when he met her at the Mesopotamian well. He would kiss it and weep and put it away again. He never forgot his family. He never forgot his children.

With all of his power and might and glory, Joseph never forgot his family, never forgot his father, never forgot his God. Prosperity doesn't have to turn us. Prosperity can help us.

As old Jacob sat there with that scarlet scarf and kissed it and put it away, he found out something; some marriages you never forget. They just get stronger.

That's the way it is, but it's not all bad to have sorrow, dear friend. That's not all bad, because sorrows of life make us better people, if we allow them to do that. Sorrows of life make us thankful for the wonderful memories of bygone days. Sorrows of life make us more considerate of others, because we're more conscious and more considerate of their needs. Sorrows of life make us more forgiving, because we all realize we're poor old sinners saved by grace. Sorrows of life make us more conscious of God and more dependent on him.

Prosperity never fazed Joseph. He never forgot God. He never got proud, and he never forgot his family. Riches may turn hearts, but it didn't turn Joseph's heart. Today we live in the same old world that Joseph lived in, with its temptations and trials of life. We have them, the same as Joseph did.

The allurements of riches are always there. The lust of the flesh is always there to torment us. The intoxication of power is just as strong as it was in Joseph's day. And so, like Joseph, let us draw close.

Let us be like Joseph and go from rags to riches, but be true to God. He wears the king's signet ring; he stamps it in soft clay or wax, and that's the royal mark. He has that mark, and he has half of the kingdom in that one ring. All that he had—beautiful, beautiful things that he had—and yet he thinks only of this wonderful God.

When I was writing about this, I thought of the thief on the cross. You know that thief on that cross—well he had been in a dungeon. Then he was taken up and put on the cross. Yet that same day, he walked the streets of paradise. From rags to riches. That thief found it, and you and I can have it, dear friends, if we just come to Jesus.

If we come to Jesus Christ and give him all that we have, receive him into our hearts, God will help us, and he'll bless us, and he'll use us. I hope that you'll do that today.

Heavenly Father, as we come to you today, we think about this story of Joseph so long ago, and how he was sold into slavery, and how by your grace and your providence and your might, you raised him up to the second highest position in all of Egypt. Through it all, he was faithful to you.

We know, Lord, that many times when people come into money and fame and fortune, they forget about you. Joseph didn't. He only shown brighter, stronger. May he be a challenge to us, Lord. Probably not many of us are going to fall into a lot of riches, but we're going to have challenging experiences in life. Maybe sometimes we'll be exalted, and sometimes put down. There will be troubles and trials.

Lord, we hear from so many every week, where a loved one is taken, a spouse is taken. It's a hard time, and no one knows what that's like unless they've experienced it. They try to empathize with us, but Lord, it's impossible. You can't know. We lose a part of our soul, it seems. We pray for these dear ones, Lord, going through great sorrow and sadness.

In those times of sadness, we draw closer to you, and we get strength and help. Heavenly Father, I pray for all those who may be on beds of sickness. I pray for the shut-ins. They're confined at home, and yet you are there. You are just as much there as you are in a church or in the great cathedrals. You're as close to them as to any of us. You love them, and you're mindful of them. Help them to realize that; help them to rejoice in the Savior.

We'll be careful to give you the thanks and praise. In Jesus' name, amen.

Moses:
Man of Many Trials

Moses:
Man of Many Trials

Deuteronomy 34:1-8

WHEN WHAT WE READ IN DEUTERONOMY 34 TAKES PLACE, Moses has led Israel out of Egypt and through the wilderness. Now they're at the border of the Promised Land, but Moses can't go into the Promised Land. God said to him, "It's time for you to come home, Moses. I want you to go to Mount Pisgah, and you can take a look at the Promised Land, but you can't go in." So Moses went up on Mount Pisgah, and he had this experience, and then God took him home:

¹ And Moses went up from the plains of Moab unto the mountain of Nebo, to the top of Pisgah, that is over against Jericho. And the Lord showed him all the land of Gilead, unto Dan,

² And all Naphtali, and the land of Ephraim, and Manasseh, and all the land of Judah, unto the utmost sea,

³ And the south, and the plain of the valley of Jericho, the city of palm trees, unto Zoar.

⁴ And the Lord said unto him, This is the land which I swore unto Abraham, unto Isaac, and unto Jacob, saying, I will give it unto thy seed: I have caused thee to see it with thine eyes, but thou shalt not go over thither.

⁵ So Moses the servant of the Lord died there in the land of Moab, according to the word of the Lord.

⁶ And he buried him in a valley in the land of Moab, over against Bethpeor: but no man knoweth of his sepulchre unto this day.

⁷ And Moses was an hundred and twenty years old when he died: his eye was not dim, nor his natural force abated.

⁸ And the children of Israel wept for Moses in the plains of Moab thirty days: so the days of weeping and mourning for Moses were ended.

Moses is a wonderful man to read about, because he inspires us and helps us. We all have troubles and trials. Sometimes as a young person, sometimes even as children, we have trials and hardships. So God says, "Comfort ye, comfort ye my people" (Isaiah 40:1). And here he comforts us through Moses, because Moses had a lot of troubles and trials, yet he stands as one of the greatest men in the whole Bible. He stands alone in the mind of the Hebrew people, because they always talked about Moses and the prophets. Moses stood out above them all.

And he had a hard life, from the cradle to the grave. He had his struggles, he had his battles, and he never gave up. When his time came to die, it was a bitter disappointment, because he couldn't go into the Promised Land. God's last word to Moses was a no. Moses wanted to go into the Promised Land, but God said, "No, Moses, you can't," because Moses had committed a sin. He had made a mark against God, and God said, "You can't go into the Promised Land. You can lead them to the border, but that's it."

The writer of the book of Hebrews talks about Moses and says, "He endured, as seeing him who is invisible" (Hebrews 11:27). Here was a man who didn't have his eyes just on the things of the earth, but on the invisible, the things of God. And that's a lesson for all of us.

We need to be very careful, because we get all taken up with the things of the earth and forget to think of the invisible. We don't think of the things of God, the things that are eternal. We shouldn't live by bread alone, but by every word of God.

Moses was that kind of a man. He could see the invisible. He could see that there was a great God, and he was going to serve him, and he did serve him all the days of his life.

So from the outside we see Moses, and how there were things that happened that we don't know about. For instance, in Jude, we have a story where the archangel Michael and the devil are disputing over the body of Moses. They were having a dispute because Moses was such a tremendous man, and if people knew where he was buried, they would have a church, they would have a monument, they would have pilgrimages to that place and they would worship that man's body. They would worship the man instead of his God. So God put him away, buried him in a special place, so that no one knows for sure. The Jewish people have a beautiful legend of how the angel of death tried in vain to take the soul of Moses from him, but he couldn't do it, though he tried every way he could to take his life. But Moses didn't die until it was in God's time and God's choosing. The legend that the Jews have says that when it came time for Moses to die, God himself came down and he drew the soul of Moses from him with a kiss; he kissed Moses into heaven. Now, I don't know if that's true or not, and it doesn't really matter. But it tells of the tenderness of God and it tells of how the heart of Moses was centered on God, and that he wanted to work and serve God in every possible way.

In many ways, when we have trials and troubles in life, it's not anything strange or new. Today, men and women have lived this way and have traveled that way, and when you think about the persecuted church, our heart goes out to the persecuted church. We pray for them and we never forget them. And so it goes—God loves us, and he tells us to just come to Jesus, come to God, put your faith in God. He loves you, and he'll help you through every trial of life.

We are very fortunate concerning Moses. We know a lot about him. There are some of the people in the Bible we don't know hardly anything about. For instance, we don't know much about Jeremiah. And what do we know about Isaiah and Paul? Very little. But with Moses, we see him from the day he was born and all of his life until the day he died.

God seems to have put great emphasis on this man and all of his life. Even when he was born, he was under the trials of Egypt, and they tried to kill him. All through life, he faced that battle.

But there was one trial Moses had that really stands out. It's a decision he had to make, and it shows his strength and his love for God.

You'll remember how Miriam came to Pharaoh's daughter and said, "Shall I get a midwife to take care of the baby?" And then she went to get her own mother, the mother of baby Moses. Pharaoh's daughter told her, "Now, you nurse him until he comes to a certain age"—probably about six years old, if we assume the tradition of that time.

Afterward, Pharaoh's daughter took young Moses to the palace, where he was trained by all the great leaders of the day, all the philosophers, and all the teachers they could possibly get for him. He lived in high luxury, and he had everything in his hands.

Then there came a day when Pharaoh called Moses in. He said something like this: "Moses, I'm coming to the end of life, but you are a strong man and a good man, and you're trained in all the knowledge of Egypt. The people admire you and follow you, they love you. So Moses, I want you to be the next Pharaoh. But in order to be the next Pharaoh, you have to renounce your heritage. You'll have to renounce the Hebrew nation. You have to tell them you don't have any part of them. You renounce them and put them away, out of your mind and out of your thoughts. And you become the next Pharaoh of Egypt."

Moses stood there, and everybody was waiting. What was Moses going to say? No one spoke and no one moved. Then after a certain length of time, there came a word from Moses as clear as a bell: "No."

Just look back at his background. His mother had him maybe five or six years; we don't know exactly the time of weaning, but it's about that age for children at that time. She taught Moses, and she said to him, when he was only a little boy, "Moses, don't ever forget that you are a Hebrew. You're not an Egyptian, you're a Hebrew, and the gods of the Egyptians are no match for Jehovah God. And don't you forget it. Though all the Hebrew people are slaves while you live in luxury in the palace, don't you forget that you are a Hebrew."

After leaving his mother, Moses was trained for all those years in the palace. He was taught everything in Egypt by the very best that Egypt had, and now he had to make a stand. And what did he say?

Well, look at Hebrews 11. It says, "By faith Moses, when he was come to years, refused to be called the son of Pharaoh's daughter; choosing rather to suffer affliction with the people of God, than to enjoy the pleasure of sin for a season; esteeming the reproach of Christ greater riches than the treasures of Egypt." Because of that decision, the name of Moses will be remembered forever.

Moses could have been buried in some great pyramid. He could have had a sepulchre like the pharaohs, maybe like that of King Tut. His pyramid would have been filled with gold and riches. He might have had other people die so they'd be with him in death; even his dog would be taken in death to go with him. Moses gave it all up. He made himself as a Hebrew. He *was* a Hebrew, and he knew that this great God Almighty, Jehovah, is the only God there is.

So Moses asked to leave. And not long after that, he was going out and he saw some of the Hebrew people and how they were being beaten, and how they were enslaved and tortured. He became so angry at one of the Egyptian men that he killed him. And Moses fled into the wilderness. He had to flee, or he would pay with his own life.

Moses was in that wilderness for forty years before he saw the burning bush. At that time, God commissioned him. But he had to wait forty years.

So maybe you are wanting to see certain things happening right now. Be patient. Just give yourself to Jesus, give yourself to God, and in all your ways, he will direct you and direct your life. You may think, "Well, nothing is happening." But just be faithful and patient and trust Jesus; walk with the Lord, and be true to him.

Moses had to be there forty years before it was time for God to come. But Moses was true to him. Moses was obedient to God.

And though he'd had all these trials, the hardest one of all I think came at the end, when he was going to be taken out of this life. We see this Moses, who's called the servant of the Lord. God looks down and he sees all that Moses has gone through, and how he has always been strong no matter what he was called upon to do.

When he was in Egypt, he was there with the people to lead them out. And he saw the ten plagues, and he led the people to the Red Sea and across the Red Sea, and he went to lead them through the wilderness. And then he came to a certain rock, and Moses knew what he was supposed to do to bring water out of the rock. However, Moses failed to follow God's instructions exactly (Numbers 20:1-13); that's when he committed the sin that God would never let him forget, and God punished him for that sin.

Moses stood at that rock and said, "You people!" He was angry with the people. So with his rod, he struck the rock twice, and out of that rock flowed the water. But that rock stood as a figure of Jesus Christ, and Jesus Christ would be struck once, but never twice. Jesus Christ was struck once, on the cross. He was put on that cross by evil hands. They nailed spikes to hold him there, and they drove the spear in his side. He was struck once, never twice.

Men treated Jesus with such evil. But you can mark this down: although evil hands tortured Jesus in the trial and the crucifixion, loving hands took him from the cross, and loving hands put him in the tomb. And enemy hands will never again touch the body of Christ. Believe me, those who are evil will tremble and they will run for the hills and ask the rocks to fall upon them, because they'll have to face an angry God, if they don't receive Jesus. God is offended, because God gave his wonderful Son. He gave the most wonderful possession he had in all the world and all of heaven.

Jesus died for you on that cross. And we trample underfoot the body of Christ, and we take his name in vain, and we don't bow our knees to Jesus Christ, and we live our life as if we're our own God. We do our own thing. We believe we're self-made men and women. Isn't that a pitiful mess? Just look what self-made people are doing to each other all over the world.

Here is this man, Jesus Christ, this wonderful Savior—struck only once.

When Moses struck that rock, and he said to Israel, "Hear you now, you rebels, must we fetch water out of this rock?"—in that moment, Moses had not honored God. He struck the rock twice with his rod.

Later, on Mount Pisgah, this came back upon Moses at the end of life. He remembered the rock. He remembered, and he pleaded with God:

"Lord God, thou has begun to show thy servant thy greatness. In thy mighty hand, I pray thee, let me go over. Let me go into that Promised Land."

He was on Pisgah, and he was going to die. He asked, "Let me go over and see the good land, the land that is beyond Jordan, that goodly mountain in Lebanon." But God said unto him, "Speak no more unto me of this matter. Get thee up unto the top of Pisgah and lift up thine eyes westward and northward and southward and eastward and behold with thine eyes, for thou shalt not go over this Jordan."

Remember that Moses was 120 years old, but his eyes were not abated. He could see just like a hawk, and he could see all that land—but he couldn't touch it. So then Moses stood on Pisgah, at the very highest peak of that mountain called Nebo. From the top of it all, he looked down and he saw all the children of Israel in all their tribes and groups, and they had their pennants flowing in the wind. They were all there by the Jordan River, ready to go into the Promised Land.

Moses could look and see how ready they were. He could see the Jordan River flowing, and we're told that it was overflowing at this time. The Jordan River is about a hundred feet wide at normal times. When it's overflowing, it can be a mile wide. Moses could see the river, and how the people were going to pass over. And from the mountaintop, he could see across the river, and he could see Jericho. And he could see with his eye of faith how that city was going to fall and be put away, and the people of Israel were going in to possess that wonderful, wonderful land. It would be *their* land.

To the south, Moses could look upon the Dead Sea. To the north, there like a jewel was the lovely little Sea of Galilee. Beyond that beautiful blue Sea of Galilee, he could see the majestic, snowcapped Mount Hermon. I've seen

Mount Hermon, and in the middle of the summer, the hottest day of the summer, you can go snow-skiing on Mount Hermon. You can go bathing and swimming in the Mediterranean Sea in the morning, and on that same day you can go up to Mount Hermon and you can ski in the afternoon.

Moses could see all those things! He could see in a distance the rocky rise called the Hill of Zion; there, on some future day, men would take the Lord Jesus to die on a cross. Maybe Moses could foresee that; maybe God let him see a glimpse of what Jerusalem would be—that holy city where the Lord Jesus was going to come—and will come again, and he's going to sit on a throne, and he's going to rule Jerusalem, and he's going to rule Israel, and he's going to rule the Middle East, and he's going to rule the whole wide world. He's going to rule personally and literally. This same Jesus is coming again!

And so there's Moses. He saw all these things, and he felt that he was going to die right there. He said, "I pray thee, let me go over and see the good land beyond the Jordan," but God said, "No. Behold with thine eyes. Thou shalt not go over."

God had decided, and that decision was never going to change. So, dear friend, it makes me think of this. We're going to come to the end of life at some time and at some place. You're going to be on Mount Pisgah, and I'm going to be on Mount Pisgah, and we're going to have to go.

Are you ready to go? Are you ready to go see God? Are you ready to meet God?

God said to Moses, "Thou shalt not go over." To those who do not know Jesus, they're not going to go over. There's no way they can pass into that Promised Land, that wonderful land. There's only one way—through the Lord Jesus Christ. And so we have to be sure we have our faith in the Lord.

As I was working on this sermon, I was thinking: Jesus wants your soul. The most precious thing you have is your soul. Jesus wants your soul. And the devil wants your soul too, so there's a battle there. Who's going to win?

You are going to choose who you're going to go with through Pisgah. Are you going to go into the Promised Land? Or are you going to go into a place of torment?

Your wife can't make that decision for you, and you can't make that decision for your children. I get letters from people who say, "My son is coming to college there, and will you talk to him? Will you give him some literature? But don't tell him that I sent you." Those parents would make that decision for that child if they could, but you can't do it.

Moses was standing on that mountain, and everything was decided. He couldn't enter that Promised Land there, right on that spot, but he was going to enter heaven and experience it there.

So you need to come to Jesus. That's our message all the time, over and over: come to the Savior.

I find often that people think that if they do more good works than bad works, they'll get to heaven. When they get to heaven's gates, God is going to measure it out, he's going to have scales there, and he's going to see if we have more good works than bad works. If so, then we go to heaven. If we have more bad works than good works, we're going to go to hell. But our works don't have a thing to do with the decision of where we will spend eternity.

Saint Paul says in the book of Romans, "But to him that worketh not but believeth is all believing." Saint Paul tells us again in Ephesians, "Not by works of righteousness which we have done, but according to his mercy, he saved us." The wonderful mercy of God! If you're counting on your own righteousness—well, God tells us through the prophet in the Old Testament that all our good works are like filthy rags—filthy, dirty, rotten rags. And you never can get them clean until you come to Jesus.

But God tells us how he's not willing that any should perish. He wants everyone to make that decision.

Jesus stands at your heart's door, and he knocks, and he's saying, "I want to come into your life. I want to cleanse you of your sins. I want to make you my child. I want to write your name in the Lamb's Book of Life. I want to give you peace. I want to give you joy."

I'm not saying he's going to give you a lot of money, because he probably won't. None of the apostles had any money. And Jesus didn't have a thing. So get money out of your head. The big things are the wonderful faith and joy and happiness and peace that only the Lord can give. Only God can give that.

So that's what we're preaching. Jesus tells us that whoever comes to him, he will in no way cast out.

I get letters from people who think they're getting in by good works. Those works don't count a thing—not a thing. They'll say, "Well, *you're* sure going to get to heaven—you've preached all these years." But my preaching won't make one particle of difference. It won't mean a thing. The only thing they're going to look for is what the death angel was looking for when he went through Egypt. He says, "When I see the blood, I'll pass over you," and if he didn't see that blood, then whether it was a man or a beast, or Egyptian or Hebrew, they died in Egypt the night of the Passover. They call it the Passover, and they celebrate it to this day, as well they should. Jesus is looking, and he's saying, "When I see the blood, I'll pass over you."

So we apply that blood by faith. We say, "Dear Jesus, please come into my heart and take away my sins." By his blood, he'll do it. His Word says, "As many as received him—Jesus—to them gave he power to become the children of God." You are never a child of God until you receive Jesus, and you'll never receive Jesus until you personally ask him into your life. Do that.

Dear Lord, we thank you for this story of Moses. What a great and tremendous man he was, and how faithful and loyal he was! He gives us courage and help and strength as we think about him and look at his life. We thank you, Lord, that he was true to you. Though he had many temptations, and though he could have made other choices, he made only one: to follow you. And that is our prayer, Lord, those of us who know you. We want to follow you until you take us home.

There's a Mount Pisgah in our life. There's a time soon when we're going to come to the end of our life, and you're going to take us home. And won't that be a glorious, wonderful day! So we live for that day. But Lord, we also think of those who don't know you, and who have no future and no hope in this world. They are going to go under the judgment of God forever, and we pray for them. I know you are talking to them, Lord; you said you draw all men onto you. You said that you're not willing that any should perish. And so you're calling them right now to come to Jesus and confess their sins and ask you to come into their life and then live for you. May there be multitudes who do that.

In Jesus' name, amen.

Samson:
Strong Man Used
by God

Samson:
Strong Man Used by God

Judges 16:23-31

[23] Then the lords of the Philistines gathered them together for to offer a great sacrifice unto Dagon their god, and to rejoice: for they said, Our god hath delivered Samson our enemy into our hand.

[24] And when the people saw him, they praised their god: for they said, Our god hath delivered into our hands our enemy, and the destroyer of our country, which slew many of us.

[25] And it came to pass, when their hearts were merry, that they said, Call for Samson, that he may make us sport. And they called for Samson out of the prison house; and he made them sport: and they set him between the pillars.

[26] And Samson said unto the lad that held him by the hand, Suffer me that I may feel the pillars whereupon the house standeth, that I may lean upon them.

[27] Now the house was full of men and women; and all the lords of the Philistines were there; and there were upon the roof about three thousand men and women, that beheld while Samson made sport.

[28] And Samson called unto the Lord, and said, O Lord God, remember me, I pray thee, and strengthen me, I pray thee, only this once, O God, that I may be at once avenged of the Philistines for my two eyes.

[29] And Samson took hold of the two middle pillars upon

which the house stood, and on which it was borne up, of the one with his right hand, and of the other with his left.

³⁰ And Samson said, Let me die with the Philistines. And he bowed himself with all his might; and the house fell upon the lords, and upon all the people that were therein. So the dead which he slew at his death were more than they which he slew in his life.

³¹ Then his brethren and all the house of his father came down, and took him, and brought him up, and buried him between Zorah and Eshtaol in the burying place of Manoah his father. And he judged Israel twenty years.

BEFORE WE LOOK AT THE OLD TESTAMENT STORY OF SAMSON, let's remember Moses who led the children of Israel in the wilderness for forty years. When Moses died, Joshua, the son of Nun, brought the children of Israel into the Promised Land, and he led them for forty years in the Promised Land, and he died at the age of 110. Then after Joshua's death, they tried to live without a leader, with everybody doing whatever was right in their own eyes. That was a total failure. So to lead the land, God raised up judges, who were really like dictators. These judges ruled for about 350 years.

There were thirteen judges in all, and the last was a man named Samson. Now, I want to say something right at the start: Samson was not as bad as people make him out to be.

I know the record of Samson's life; it was a life of dissipation, of sensuality and recklessness. Most of the time he was just more of a juvenile than anything else. But by the same token, Samson was one of the greatest judges Israel ever had.

Don't forget that Samson is included in Hebrews 11, which is God's register of the great outstanding men and women of the Bible. Verse 32 says, "And what shall I more say? For the time will fail me to tell of Gideon and of Barak and of Samson and of Jephthae, of David also, and Samuel, and of the prophets."

Samson—in spite of escapades, in spite of his foolishness and sins— had a place in his heart for God. He had a basic love for God. He never forgot his God. He was used of God; never forget that.

We can divide his life into three chapters. Each chapter begins with a woman, and not a very nice woman. As a matter of fact, terrible women.

How he found them, I don't know. But he struck out with each one of them. They say three strikes and you're out; with Samson, it's three women and you're out. It just seems like he fell in love with these women and couldn't control himself. They were the objects of his affection, or maybe we should say they were the lusts of his flesh. Let's look at these women.

Samson found woman number one when he was about twenty years of age. He found her in Philistine territory, which was enemy territory. As a matter of fact, all three women that Samson fell in love with were Philistines. Apparently, he couldn't find an Israelite woman he liked; he had to get a Philistine.

On one of his trips into Philistine territory, he went to a town called Timnah, and there he found a woman who seemed the most beautiful thing he ever laid eyes. He went home and told his parents, "Get her for me as my wife."

Samson's parents are sick. They said, "Look, she has a different faith, a different belief. She worships idols. Besides, aren't there pretty women in Israel?" But no, Samson refused. He had to have the Philistine. He said that if he didn't have her, he was going to die.

Where have I heard that before? As a matter of fact, I felt that way when I saw Beulah: *if I don't get Beulah as my wife, I'm going to die.* I think I might have, so God gave her to me. How she ever married me—that's a whole other story.

Samson was determined to marry this woman. On one of his trips to Timnah to see her, a lion raised up in front of him, and the Spirit came upon Samson, and with superhuman strength, he took that lion by the jaw and ripped him to pieces.

Some time later, when Samson returned, he came across the lion's carcass. By now, the vultures had feasted on it, and the ants had cleaned away what the vultures didn't eat, and nothing was left but bones. A swarm of bees had filled that carcass with honey. Samson ate some of the honey, then went on to the marriage. Now, in those days, it took several days, even weeks, as they prepared and got ready for the marriage.

While they were waiting, Samson gave a party for thirty of the young Philistine men. At this party he said, "I'll give you a riddle, and if you can answer the riddle, I'll give you thirty plain robes and thirty fancy robes." That was a plain robe and a fancy robe for each of them if they could answer Samson's riddle. They answered him, "Give us the riddle; we'll take you on."

This is the riddle he gave: "Out of the eater, something to eat. Out of the strong, something sweet."

For three days, they tried to figure out that riddle, and they absolutely couldn't. On the fourth day, they went to the woman Samson was going to marry, and they said, "You get the answer for this riddle, and if you don't, we're going to burn down your house with all your family."

The woman talked to Samson, and she begged him for the answer for seven days. After seven days, he gave her the answer, and she told the young Philistine men. So Samson lost his bet.

Where was Samson going to get sixty robes? Easy. He went to Ashkelon, a Philistine village, and he killed thirty young men, took their garments, brought them back, and paid off his debt.

He was really angry now, and because of this, he walked out on the wedding. When the time for the ceremony came, no Samson. The bride's father said, "Well, this girl is going to get married. So we'll marry her to the best man." So she became another man's wife.

Later that year, at the time of the wheat harvest, Samson had a change of heart. He said, "I think I'll go back and marry that girl at Timnah." When he got back there, the woman's father stopped Samson from seeing her. He told Samson, "You're out of luck, because I gave her to the best man. There's nothing you can do. But she has a younger sister, and she's prettier anyway."

Samson was angry again. He took three foxes, tied their tails together, placed a torch on their tails, set them on fire, and turned the foxes loose. Those three hundred foxes ran through the Philistine fields and vineyards and orchards, burning all the crops.

That precipitated war between the Philistines and the Israelites, although the Israelites didn't want this war, because the Philistines were too powerful. Then the Philistines said, "Deliver this man to us, Samson, and we won't have war with you. Otherwise, we'll fight."

Samson was tied up with new ropes, and the Israelites brought him out bound. But when the Philistines came shouting to take him, the Spirit of the Lord rushed upon Samson. The ropes that were binding him just melted away, like cloth on fire. Then Samson found a donkey's jawbone and grabbed it for a weapon. He killed a thousand Philistines on the spot. Then he said, "With a donkey's jawbone, I have made donkeys of them. With a donkey's jawbone, I have killed a thousand men." Then he threw away the jawbone, and that ended the story of woman number one.

Woman number two entered the picture when Samson went to Gaza and saw a prostitute. He decided to spend the night with her. When the rulers of Gaza heard that Samson was in town, they are thrilled. They locked the city gates, and they planned to ambush and kill him once the light of morning arrived. Samson would have no way of escape.

But around midnight, Samson got sick of the whole deal and decided to leave. He packed up and walked out. He came to the city gates and found them bolted shut as tightly as they could be. Samson lost his temper again, and he grabbed the bolts and the pillars and the gates and ripped them all out. He put all this on his shoulders, and carried everything to a hill facing Hebron, forty miles away. And that ended the story of woman number two.

Then we come to woman number three. Her name was Delilah. She was a Philistine like the other two. Samson made a trip to the Valley of Sorek, and true to form, he fell in love with Delilah.

When the Philistine leaders found out about this, they came and said, "All right Delilah, listen. You just get with him, and you find out the secret of his great strength, so that we can come and overpower him and capture him. When you do that, each of us will give you eleven hundred pieces of silver." In those days, that was a fortune.

Delilah sold out. She was ready for business. She kept asking Samson to tell her his secret, but Samson played games with her and gave her wrong information. Delilah was fooled, and she passed along his answer each time to the Philistines. They would come rushing in to take him, and Delilah would cry out, "Samson, the Philistines are upon you!" But each time, no matter what they tried, they couldn't capture Samson. He always broke free.

Delilah didn't give up. She kept nagging Samson until he was almost ready to die. Finally he told her the secret. "I'm a Nazirite. Cut off my hair, and I lose my power."

Delilah knew just what to do next. Clarence Macartney tells us:

> With flattery and caresses and wine, she puts Samson to sleep. While he slumbers across her lap, a Philistine comes in. No doubt, handling his razor with fear and trembling, he shaves the head of Samson, the wonderful golden-sunlight locks falling at the feet of Delilah.

Then she shouts for the fourth time, "The Philistines are upon you!" And Samson said, "I'll do to them as I did before." But alas, he didn't realize that God's Spirit had left him. His mighty power was gone, and the Philistines took him captive. They took him to Gaza, and with red-hot irons they burned out his eyes. They put him on a mill with the slaves to grind out corn.

And there you have the picture of this great and mighty man with his eyes now gone, and he's grinding out corn at a mill like a lowly donkey. It makes you want to weep.

That's not the end of the story. Samson's hair grew back, but the Philistines didn't notice, or if they did notice, they didn't care. He was their slave. But his locks of hair came back, long and thick and beautiful like before.

Then came a day, a special day, and they're going to have a celebration for their god, Dagon. Three thousand people come up to the temple of Dagon, and several thousand others in the court below. There's an open courtyard, and in full view of all the people, into this open courtyard, Samson was led by a little boy—not a warrior, but a little boy, leading that giant.

The people had come to honor their god because clearly their god Dagon was greater than Israel's God, since Dagon had delivered Samson into their hands. They wanted to make sport of him, to mock him, to laugh at him. They wanted to degrade him, and to torture him in a certain way. And they wanted to celebrate.

John Milton in his poem "Samson Agonistes," puts Samson's plight exactly when he describes him as "eyeless in Gaza, at the mill with slaves." That was Samson.

Macartney has a beautiful passage on this:

> Now, here comes Samson led by the land. The spectators crowding the roof garden of the temple and palace. Come, enter with amazement upon the magnificent proportions of the blind giant. Look at those legs like bronze pillars, and those shoulders like two hills, and the neck like a bull of Bashan, and that back, those great arms and hands. But now his eye is out; he's helpless, and they taunt, and they laugh, and they make sport of him.

The powerful Samson led by that little boy, and imagine all the whooping and hollering. Samson was disgraced, and he's blind, and he's humiliated.

Then Samson tells the little boy, "I'm getting very weary, and I need to get into the shade. Perhaps you could lead me by the main pillars of the temple and let me sit in the shade there for a few moments."

The little boy led Samson, and he sat between the pillars. On the roof above there are three thousand people, and thousands more are inside the temple. Then Samson put his arms around the great temple pillars.

This isn't in the Bible, but I think it's true. Samson said, "Little boy, get out of here. Run to your mama as fast as you can run. Now get." The little boy ran as fast as he could run.

Then Samson, with his long hair flowing over his shoulders, his empty eye sockets turned toward heaven, said a prayer. "O Lord God, remember me, I pray thee. Strengthen me, I pray thee, only this once, O God, that I may at once avenge the Philistines for my two eyes."

The half-drunken crowd looked at him and said, "Look there, Samson is resting." What they didn't know was that Samson wasn't resting, he was praying.

And after he prayed, he tightened those arms around those two pillars, and he lifted them from their pedestals. With a sickening noise, the whole temple crashed down. At one time, three thousand Philistines were killed, including all the Philistine leaders, and probably Delilah, though we don't know.

I want you to think about that prayer of Samson when he prayed, "Lord God, remember me, I pray thee. Strengthen me only this once." That was the final prayer of Samson. As wayward and sinful as Samson was, he never forgot God. He always had time for God, and he knew that his strength really came from God. He knew that he had sinned, and he knew he'd wandered from God. Grinding at the slave mills in Gaza, Samson had a lot of time to think and to reflect. And though his eyes were blind, he saw his God. That's repentance, and that's Samson's final prayer. God answered that prayer. Even in his death, Samson gave great service to the people of God over their archenemies, the Philistines.

And so it was that in his repentance, Samson prayed "only this once." Have you ever thought of how many people, like Samson, look to God "only this once"?

You think about Peter and his life, and how three times he swore he didn't know Jesus. Then all of a sudden, he saw Jesus, who'd been lacerated and scourged and mocked, and he was bleeding. And the Bible says that Jesus turned and looked upon Peter.

Peter was cut to his heart, in an act of sorrow and repentance. Just that one time, it was Peter; just this one time, he prayed to God to forgive him, and God forgave him.

Think of Saint Paul on his way to Damascus, intending to persecute the people of God. Then, on the road to Damascus, that blinding light struck him down and made him blind. He experienced the vision and the voice of Jesus; only this one time it happened. But from only that one time, Paul replied and said, "Lord, what wilt thou have me to do?" Paul became the greatest servant God ever had, and he wrote most of the New Testament.

Or think of the prodigal son who demanded his inheritance from his father, then he went out and squandered it all. In his hunger he was eating the husks with the hogs, till finally, only this once, he came to himself and he said, "I will arise and go to my father's house."

That was an act of repentance. It was a prayer of only this one time in the prodigal's life that brought him back home, back to his father.

There was the thief on the cross who did the same thing when he saw the Lord Jesus Christ. He had lived a terrible life, crime after crime. He had punishment coming to him. He was being crucified, and as he was dying on his cross, he first rebuked the other crucified thief who had reproached Jesus, and then he said, "Jesus, Lord, remember me when thou comest into thy kingdom." He had one chance, just this once, and he became the first person to enter paradise after the crucifixion with Jesus.

Maybe you have slipped away from God; maybe you've yielded into some temptation, like Samson did.

"Only this once" assures you of the forgiveness of God. If we repent, if we turn to Jesus, if we call upon his name, he will freely forgive. Just as he came again to Samson with the power of the Holy Spirit, he will come to you in your repentance by the Holy Spirit, and he'll baptize you into the body of Christ. You can become his child.

God will freely forgive you, if you come to him. Now, the world doesn't do it that way. The world's attitude is that whatsoever a man sows, that shall he also reap. The world's way is an eye for an eye and a tooth for a tooth, and I'll settle the score. What I've written, I've written, and I'll never change my mind, and I'll never turn. Your sins will find you out. That's the world's way; that's not the gospel.

Let me tell you what the gospel is. The gospel is, "Believe on the Lord Jesus Christ, and thou shalt be saved" (Acts 16:31). The gospel is, "As many as received him, to them gave he power to become the children of God" (John 1:12). The gospel is, "Whosoever believeth in him should not perish, but have everlasting life" (John 3:16).

The gospel is, "Whosoever shall call upon the name of the Lord shall be saved" (Romans 10:13).

The gospel is, "Though your sins be as scarlet, they shall be as white as snow, though they be red like crimson; they shall be as wool" (Isaiah 1:18).

The gospel is, "As far as the east is from the west, so far hath he removed our transgressions from us" (Psalm 103:12).

The gospel is, "Their sins and inequities will I remember no more" (Hebrews 8:12).

The gospel is, "Wherefore also he is able to save to the uttermost them that draw near unto God through him" (Hebrews 7:25).

The gospel is, "The blood of Jesus his Son cleanseth us from all sin" (1 John 1:7).

Only this once—and your sins can be taken away, and your name can be written in the Lamb's Book of Life. You can be saved from the torments of hell, which are literal and are real.

Right now may be your "once"; it may be your only opportunity to come to Jesus Christ—right this hour, right this minute.

Do you remember the story when Jesus went through Jericho, and there was a blind beggar named Bartimaeus who cried out to Jesus? Bartimaeus wanted to be healed. But the people tried to silence him and keep him from coming to Jesus. They didn't want him to bother Jesus. And Bartimaeus could have said, "Well, I guess maybe I'll wait until another day," or, "I'll wait until there aren't so many people around," or, "I'll wait until my birthday," or, "I'll wait until Jesus comes again—then I'll know for sure." He might have said any of those things. But let me tell you, Jesus Christ never came to Jericho again. This was Bartimaeus's first chance and last chance.

And Bartimaeus made the most of it. When they tried to silence him, we read that "he cried the more a great deal, Thou Son of David, have mercy on me." Then we read, "And Jesus stood still, and commanded him to be called." Bartimaeus rose and came to Jesus, and Jesus healed him.

This moment might be your last. You might be like Bartimaeus, and you may never have another chance. I don't know. But I'll tell you what I do know. I know that eventually we'll come to that day when it *is* our last chance.

Only this once.

Years ago I read about a nineteenth-century passenger ship called the *Stephen Whitney,* that had sailed across the Atlantic from America. But in a storm, it crashed into rocks off the coast of Ireland, with her bow stuck on a rocky ledge. The ship's officers gave the order to abandon the ship. They said, "Escape with your life. The ship is going down."

A few people jumped from the ship immediately and were saved, but most waited a moment, putting it off. Then all of a sudden, a surge from the sea took the ship off the ledge, and it quickly sank; everyone still on board was lost.

Only this once—this once of repentance, this once of prayer, this once. If you'll repent and believe, you'll live forever. I pray that you come to Jesus, and that you come just as you are.

Heavenly Father, when we read Samson's story, our heart aches. This man had such potential and great possibilities, and he threw it away living selfishly. Dear God, he was taken by enemies and his eyes put out.

But we thank you that he repented of his sins, and his life closes with the power he once had coming back, more powerful than before. He avenged the enemies of God as he went to his death.

I pray that as we think of this story of Samson, it will lead many people to a faith in Jesus Christ—many who have been thinking about such a commitment, and many who keep putting it off. I pray that in the preaching of the word there would be many who will call upon your name and be saved today.

And I pray that Christian people everywhere will be encouraged when they see that there is a great God who never forgets us; even though we sin, he never forgets his people. When we repent, he freely forgives and restores.

Use these words to honor Jesus and to honor yourself, heavenly Father. May all glory be yours.

In your name we pray, amen.

David:

Great Sinner, Great Saint

6

David:
Great Sinner, Great Saint

1 Samuel 17:45-51

[45] Then said David to the Philistine, Thou comest to me with a sword, and with a spear, and with a shield: but I come to thee in the name of the Lord of hosts, the God of the armies of Israel, whom thou hast defied.

[46] This day will the Lord deliver thee into mine hand; and I will smite thee, and take thine head from thee; and I will give the carcasses of the host of the Philistines this day unto the fowls of the air, and to the wild beasts of the earth; that all the earth may know that there is a God in Israel.

[47] And all this assembly shall know that the Lord saveth not with sword and spear: for the battle is the Lord's, and he will give you into our hands.

[48] And it came to pass, when the Philistine arose, and came, and drew nigh to meet David, that David hastened, and ran toward the army to meet the Philistine.

[49] And David put his hand in his bag, and took thence a stone, and slang it, and smote the Philistine in his forehead, that the stone sunk into his forehead; and he fell upon his face to the earth.

[50] So David prevailed over the Philistine with a sling and with a stone, and smote the Philistine, and slew him; but there was no sword in the hand of David.

[51] Therefore David ran, and stood upon the Philistine, and took his sword, and drew it out of the sheath thereof, and slew him, and cut off his head therewith. And when the Philistines saw their champion was dead, they fled.

WE LOOK NOW AT A MAN WHO HAD GREAT SINS—and he found salvation. The man's name is David, one of the great giants of the Old Testament.

Many books have been written about David. He stands head and shoulders above the leaders of his day or any other day. The sad thing about David is that in the world, he's known only as an adulterer and a murderer. That's what they like to hang on him. They make a big deal out of it. That's the way of the world. If you do something wrong, if you commit some sin, they like to hang it on you. But if you have virtue and if you do good, very little is said about that.

What do we care what the world says, or what people say? We want to know what God has to say. He is the one we're ultimately going to answer to some day. I'm not going to answer to any man; I'm going to answer to Jesus Christ, who will judge all the believers and all the unbelievers in their time.

So when we read about David, we read something that's very beautiful and something kind of startling, because God tells us that he was a man after God's own heart. That's not said about any other person in the Bible. David was a man after God's own heart. And that simply means that David is right with God, that he's come to God and found forgiveness and been cleansed of his sins. He didn't know anything about Jesus Christ, because Jesus had not yet come into the world and gone to the cross to pay for the sins of the world. David believed in God as Abraham did. David believed God, and he was obedient to God, and he trusted God—put his faith in God—and this was counted to him for righteousness.

Now, after the cross, we have to do more than that. We have to do more than just believe in God. We have to believe in Jesus Christ. Remember in John 14, where Jesus tells his disciples that he's going to go away, and they were troubled. He said to them, "Let not your heart be troubled. You believe in God, *believe also in me.*" You've got to believe in Jesus. Everybody believes in God, but you have to believe in Jesus, who's the Savior of the world.

So this wonderful David is one who has found salvation, as he put his faith in God Almighty and trusted him fully.

The name David means "beloved," probably in the sense of "beloved of Jehovah." David was born in Bethlehem. He was the great-grandson of Ruth and Boaz. He was of the tribe of Judah, and his father's name was Jesse. He had seven brothers, and he was the youngest.

Jesus is often referred to as the son of David. Jesus also talked about himself as being of the seed of David. In the book of Revelation, Jesus says, "I am the root and the offspring of David."

David was a handsome young man. Scripture says that he was ruddy (in 1 Samuel 16:1). That might mean that he had red hair. We don't know that for sure, but we do know that he was outstanding in appearance. He was handsome, and he was brave, and he was true.

David was a shepherd for his father during his boyhood, and he was musically gifted with the harp to perfection. He was a singer. As a matter of fact, he was such a good singer, they called him "the sweet singer of Israel."

He was a brave man. We're told that as a young shepherd, he killed both a lion and a bear in defense of his flock.

While David was still a shepherd boy, the great prophet Samuel came to his town and anointed him. He said, "Now this boy is going to be the king of Israel." David was just a lad, a shepherd boy coming out of the fields.

Then many years passed. But in God's own time, David became the king of Israel, and a great one at that.

At the time, there was already a king over Israel, and his name was Saul. Saul was disobedient to God. The Bible tells us that Saul failed to listen to God, and was so disobedient that God took his Spirit from him.

When he took his Spirit from him, Saul was on his own. As a consequence, he suffered melancholy and jealously and hatred. As time went on, evil spirits began to work in his heart, and he became so evil that he wanted to kill David. One time, he threw a spear at David, but God spared David's life. King Saul became a desperately wicked man.

We read on in David's story about his ordeal with Goliath. David came to help his three brothers who were serving in the army. In that day, families fed the soldiers; the armies did not have these big cookouts and all, so the families took care of their boys, and they'd send food to them while they're serving as soldiers.

When David got there, he saw this giant named Goliath, who was making fun of the God of Israel and desecrating his name. And because Goliath was so huge, nobody would go and fight him. But David said, "I will fight him."

So David fought him, and he won this great victory over Goliath. As a result, he was the hero in all of Israel. Everybody was talking about him. We're told in the Scriptures that people were singing a song that had these words: "Saul has slain his thousands, David his ten thousands." How do you suppose that set with Saul? Saul was so angry about it that he would've killed David. But Jonathan—Saul's son and David's friend—came into the picture, and Jonathan helped David and watched over him to keep him safe.

Eventually, King Saul died. He died by his own hand on Mount Gilboa. Saul was a man who in physical form was a head taller than anybody in Israel, and God gave everything into his hands. But Saul disobeyed God; he wouldn't listen to God. He was headstrong and proud—so God set him aside.

God will do that today if we get proud and think we're so great. God will set us aside. He'll take somebody else. We're not the only one in the picture; God has many that he can choose from.

Once Saul was dead, David went to Hebron in the hill country in Judah, about nineteen miles southwest of Jerusalem. They made him king of just one tribe, the tribe of Judah. David ruled over Judah for seven and a half years. Over time, he fought many battles and put down all of enemies. He put down the Philistines, the Moabites, the Ammonites, the Edomites, and the Amalekites, and he made his kingdom strong until finally they said, "We're going to put him in Jerusalem." And he became king of all Israel. The first thing he did was to move the Ark of the Covenant to Jerusalem. He ruled Israel for forty years.

We want to look at David's life, to see what lessons we can learn from him.

The first lesson is that disobedience carries a very high price tag, and that can be seen in David's life. For example, in his sin with Bathsheba and his disobedience to God, a sin that has followed him for three thousand years. When people talk about David, they'll talk about Bathsheba all the time.

But David was forgiven because he was repentant, and his sin was taken away. And I don't care what your sin is. David had terrible sins, but he was white as snow. "Wash me and I shall be whiter than snow"—that's what God will do for you.

I know I hear people many times who'll say, "I've sinned too much; I know God won't forgive me." And they will say, "I knew it was wrong, and I did it anyway. If I didn't know, if I'd done it in ignorance, then I can see God forgiving me. But I knew it was wrong, and I did it anyway."

But I'm here to tell you there's such a thing called the grace of God. Of all the religions in the world, only Christianity has grace. And grace simply means that God has given us favor and he blesses us, though we don't deserve it. God made forgiveness possible for us, no matter what our sins are—if we come repentant to him, and receive his Son as our Savior. We're washed clean, our names are put in the Lamb's Book of Life, and God says, "Their sins and inequities will I remember no more."

David of course had that wonderful, wonderful relationship with God, just as we have that relationship with Jesus Christ. It's all because we come to him by faith, and ask for forgiveness, and ask him to help us.

David had some sins, and when he had that sin with Bathsheba, and he prayed that God would forgive him, I want to point out that David said, "Restore unto me the joy of my salvation." I want you to be sure of this, friends: don't ever think that David lost his salvation. He didn't say, "Restore unto me my salvation." If you're saved, you can't lose it. But David says, "Restore unto me the *joy* of my salvation." We can lose the fellowship with God and the joy of salvation if we have unconfessed sins.

We're saved and we're walking with the Lord, as I am here. At ten years old, I accepted the Lord, and when I commit a sin of jealousy or envy or pride or whatever it is, then I lose the joy of that salvation. I don't lose the salvation, I lose the joy. And then when I confess my sins to Jesus, then I'm doing as he says in 1 John 1:9—that if we confess our sins, he'll forgive us our sins and cleanse us from all unrighteousness. Then we have that joy back again.

It's just like if you're married, and you say something harsh to your wife, and you don't feel good about it, and you won't feel good about it until you tell her you're sorry. Or you're angry with a friend. You said something you shouldn't have said, and the joy of that friendship is missing until you go and tell him you're sorry.

So if you sin, go and tell the Lord that you're sorry. Confess to him that you were wrong, and restore the joy of your salvation.

This tells us that we need to be careful—first of all, to be careful that we walk with the Lord, because disobedience is a bad thing, and it causes a lot of grief. The second thing is to realize that faith can conquer any obstacle.

David, when caring for his father's sheep, encountered a lion and a bear that had come to destroy the flock. He was able to kill both of them with the help of the Lord. That encounter gave him great faith, and he knew that God was on his side, and that he could beat any foe there was. That's why when we're with the Lord and he helps us, and we know it's the hand of the Lord that has helped us, we're not to forget how God helped us in this special way. Don't forget when you have victories over your sins, over your temptation, or whatever it might be. Just remember that God is helping you, and remember the good things he did for you.

We're told that when David slew Goliath, he took Goliath's armor and put it in his tent. Why did he do that? To brag? No, he did that so he would never forget what God had done and how God helped him.

When God has helped us, keep your mind on that, and remember that, and it'll help you with the next battle. That's the way it was with David. He had killed the lion and the bear, so what was a giant? God was helping with that. David remembered, and it helped him to take care of Goliath.

We need to lean on the Lord and remember that God will help us, whatever battle we might have. We're all going to face a battle, it's going to come to us, and when we come to those things, we're going to need extra help; we can't achieve victory by ourselves.

Remember when David was going to fight with Goliath, and his brothers told him he was crazy. His brothers said, "You can't do that." And this is what David said: "When I'm taking care of my father's sheep, and a lion or a bear comes and grabs a lamb from the flock, I go after that lion or bear with a club, and I take the lamb from his mouth. If he turns on me, I catch him by the jaw and club him to death. I've done this to both lions and bears, and I'll do it to this heathen Philistine. He has defied the armies of the living God. The Lord who saved me from the claws and teeth of the lion and the bear will save me from the Philistine."

David never forgot that, and he put that armor there. He never forgot how he killed the lion and the bear—and the giant.

So think back of how God has helped you. There have been times when you didn't know what to do. There have been times when only later you could see that you could've been killed in a car accident. It's that close. It could've happened, but it didn't happen. God is watching over us.

Just put your faith in this wonderful Lord. You're going to have giants to face and to fight as you travel along. You're going to face the giant of fear. Maybe you're fearing old age. I never fear old age, because I'm ninety-five, so why would I fear it? I'm in it. It isn't too bad. I slowed down a little bit, but I just have a wonderful time. And I have a walker. I get along with a walker, and everybody opens the doors for me, and they say hello to me, and they help me carry my groceries too, and they are just so wonderful. I wouldn't part with that walker for anything. Don't worry about old age. You gotta get there first.

Sometimes people will face the giant of loneliness. It will come, and we hear from people all the time who say, "I don't have any friends, I don't have anybody to talk to, I'm the loneliest person in the world." That's a giant to face.

There's the giant of poverty, when you can't pay your bills, and you have your children to support. How are you going to clothe your children and take care of them?

Those giants will come. Giants of liquor and drugs and illicit sex. There are giants in the land, and David would cry out and say to us, "Just have faith in God; never waver, never fear, never doubt. God is there. He has all power. Take heart, stand tall. Faith can win every victory."

Something else I think David would tell us. He would say, Guard the eye gate. Watch out what you're watching, what you're looking at." For David, that was his downfall. He looked upon this woman, and he lusted after her, and he couldn't get it out of his head. It just consumed him, and led him to terrible sins.

Watch out what you put into your mind. You can so put something in your mind just like that—but you can't take it out so easily.

I remember we had hired men, and I remember some of the cuss words they used. That's eighty, ninety years ago. Some of the sights that you see and the things that you hear—that's why you need to be careful what you watch on your television. Watch the eye gate. Satan is constantly there to put something destructive into your heart and mind. Be careful of the television and videos and movies you watch, and of the literature and the pictures that you look at, and of the friends you have and the company that you keep. Because once you'll put something there in your mind, it won't be so easy to take it out again.

We need to have a constant guard over that. David is telling us to keep our eyes open and to be careful what we watch. David would heartily agree with Saint Paul, who said the very same thing:

> Finally brethren, whatsoever things are true, whatsoever things are honest, whatsoever things are just, whatsoever things are pure, whatsoever things are lovely, whatsoever things are of good report, if there be any virtue, any praise, think on these things. (Philippians 4:8)

Yes, watch your eye gate.

Finally, learn to wait on God.

When you read about David, here he is just a little shepherd boy, and Samuel the great prophet comes and anoints him, and he says, "You're going to be king of Israel." But David had to wait. And he waited for years, waited and waited, and finally he was king, but only of the one tribe of Judah.

Eventually, with God's own time, he would get to be king over all Israel. But for seven and a half years at Hebron, he was king only of Judah. He was supposed to be king of all Israel, but he was king of just a few people there. David would tell us today to wait on the Lord, to be of good courage and wait on the Lord. Don't force things. Give God time. Wait and let God. Just learn to trust Jesus. Learn to give him everything you have. Wait on the Lord. He knows when the best time is. He has the timetable from eternity. Just lean on Jesus.

John Stallings wrote this little chorus:

> I'm learning to lean, learning to lean,
>
> learning to lean on Jesus,
>
> finding more power than I'd ever dreamed.
>
> I'm learning to lean on Jesus.
>
> The joy I can't explain fills my heart
>
> since the day I made Jesus my king.
>
> His blessed Holy Spirit is leading my way.
>
> He's teaching, and I'm learning to lean.[5]

Thank God for the great King David. This man of God blundered and sinned terribly. Yet in his heart, in his soul, he trusted God. He loved God and wanted to serve God, and God looks upon the heart and not the mistakes we've made. When we sin, we may commit a sin that just is not really as of us; we just had a moment without thinking, or whatever we're at, and we may commit some sin, and God knows that isn't our heart.

You see, other people don't know that about us. They just see how we live, and they judge us. But God looks at the heart, and if your heart is right, if your heart keeps right, God will help you and he'll bless you and use you, and that's what he did with David. Never forget the forgiveness of God. Never forget that grace of God, because God tells us, "My grace is sufficient for thee." In other words, he's telling us, "I don't care what your sins are, I'll just wash them away. My grace and my salvation will cover all your sins."

I also want to warn you about something. I had somebody tell me not too long ago, "Well, I'm going to be a Christian. I want to be a good one.

I'm going to straighten up my life, and then I'm going to come to Jesus." But that's the devil's idea. Because you'll never get straightened up enough, and you'll go to hell trying to get straightened up and cleaned up on your own.

So you just come, as dirty as you are, with all the sins of the world, and all the sins you've committed in the world, and just ask God to forgive you. God says that though your sins be as scarlet, he'll take them away.

Jesus tells us in John 5:24, "Verily, verily, I say unto you, he that heareth my word, and believeth on him that sent me, hath everlasting life, and shall not come into condemnation; but is passed from death unto life." The minute you trust Jesus, you are born again. You're born from above. Your name's written in the Lamb's Book of Life. You're baptized by the Holy Spirit into the body of Christ. You have eternal life, and you will never perish. That happens the moment you accept Jesus and I just pray that you'll do that.

Don't put it off, because you'll never get it done. Sometimes people say, "I'm going to wait and do it on my birthday." Or a husband will say, "I'll do it on our anniversary and make my wife happy." Well, on your anniversary you'll probably be out fishing. Who knows what you'll be doing? And you may not even be here, because God tells us not to count on tomorrow, because tomorrow may never come. You don't have yesterday, and you don't have tomorrow—all you have is today, right now. Come to Jesus now.

God tells us in 1 John 1:9 that the blood of Jesus Christ his Son cleanses us from all sin. He tells us, "I'll forgive your sins."

I have people writing me and saying, "I can't forgive myself." You know, that's the devil just making you worry. God says, "I'll remember them no more." If God doesn't remember your sins, why should you?

Just pray, "Dear Jesus, I'm a sinner. I ask you to come into my heart and take away my sins, and I'll make you the Lord of my life. I'll serve you the best I can." And then you thank him, and then you tell somebody.

Dear heavenly Father, thank you for the story of David, this shepherd boy who had no armor, no spear, no shield, but he had you. And that's all he needed. The Philistine giant came to meet him, but David ran to meet the giant. We thank you for this story. Help us to know, dear God, that when you want something done, it will be done; that you have all power and might, and we're safe in your hands, and we fight in the name of the Lord. We fight the devil and sin and wickedness, and we're going to prevail.

When we go to your book, the Bible, we read that last chapter and we see the consummation of all time. We see that the great God of Jacob and Isaac, that great God Almighty, is the ruler of all of the world. And when the world will be dissolved in flames, there'll be a new Jerusalem. We can be a part of that if we have Jesus. Thank you for Jesus. May everyone reading this be sure they put their faith in Jesus right now.

We're praying that absolutely every one places their faith in you, that they make the prayer of the penitent: "God be merciful to me, a sinner. Save me for Christ's sake."

That's our prayer, in Jesus' name. Amen.

Elijah:
Great Man Who Stood for God

7

Elijah:
Great Man Who Stood for God

1 Kings 18:36-39

In 1 Kings 18 we find a story of Elijah. There had been a famine in the land and a drought in the land. There was going to be a great meeting on Mount Carmel where Elijah would challenge the priests of Baal—850 of them against one man! Both parties were going to pray for fire to come down and consume the offerings they had prepared.

The 850 priests of Baal went through all their attempts all day long, but no fire came. Then we read this, beginning in 1 Kings 18:36:

> ³⁶ And it came to pass at the time of the offering of the evening sacrifice, that Elijah the prophet came near, and said, Lord God of Abraham, Isaac, and of Israel, let it be known this day that thou art God in Israel, and that I am thy servant, and that I have done all these things at thy word.
>
> ³⁷ Hear me, O Lord, hear me, that this people may know that thou art the Lord God, and that thou hast turned their heart back again.
>
> ³⁸ Then the fire of the Lord fell, and consumed the burnt sacrifice, and the wood, and the stones, and the dust, and licked up the water that was in the trench.
>
> ³⁹ And when all the people saw it, they fell on their faces: and they said, The Lord, he is the God; the Lord, he is the God.

I love Elijah. He was a grand, great man of God, and he stood alone for God, and you just can't help but admire him.

His name means, "My God is Jehovah." But we hardly know anything about his background. We don't know anything about his family or about his birth. We know he was called a Tishbite, and that means that he came from Tishbe in Gilead. And that's all we know about Elijah's background and home.

It seems that he may have been advanced in years when he came to the scene that we're looking at in 1 Kings 18, where he challenges the prophets of Baal on Mount Carmel and has that great victory. He may be a little bit older, but we really don't know, and it really doesn't matter.

Elijah was a recluse, living away from the cities. He lived out in the wilderness somewhere, who knows where. He wore a mantle made of horse hair or camel's hair, and he had a girdle made of leather tied around his waist. He wore the garb of a prophet because a prophet he was.

At the time Elijah lived, Israel's religious life was in a crisis. They had a king whose name was Ahab and who had a wife named Jezebel. And don't name your little girls Jezebel; don't even name your dog Jezebel, because she was a very wicked woman. She was a Canaanite, and she worshiped the false god Baal. Under Jezebel's strong influence and King Ahab's weakness (I guess he was afraid of her or something), she brought in the worship of Baal, and it swept the whole land of Israel. Jezebel appointed priests and prophets of Baal in multitude. She also put out a death warrant for all the prophets of Jehovah. Many of those prophets were killed outright, and others had to hide in caves in the mountains.

It just seemed like the worship of Jehovah, so far as Israel was concerned, was going to perish from the land. Only seven thousand believers remained in the entire land of Israel. We know that because God says there were seven thousand who hadn't bent the knee to Baal.

But suddenly, out of nowhere, Elijah came on the scene, and he came to King Ahab and stood right before him, looking him in the eye. And he told Ahab something like this: "Just as surely as the God of Israel lives, there's going to be a famine, because there won't be any rain for several years." And he said, "It isn't going to rain until I say the word."

Then God told Elijah, "Go, leave Ahab now; you've given him the message, you stood before the king. Now go to a place called the Brook Cherith, and stay there." This would be on the east side of the Jordan River, near where that river enters into the Dead Sea. And God told Elijah, "I've commanded the ravens, and they will bring you food to eat without fail." And that is exactly what he did. It just shows you the great faith of Elijah.

He was sitting by that little brook out there in the wilderness. He had only that brook for his water, and his only food was what those birds happened to fly in with. It shows us that God is a God of nature. He told a giant fish to swallow Jonah, and he told the birds to take food to Elijah. He talks to the wind, and the wind stops, and the sea is calm. This is the God of creation. All of creation listens to him and obeys him. So here came the birds, and Elijah was fed every morning and every evening. The ravens always appeared.

Just like Elijah told Ahab, there was no rain and there was no dew throughout all the land. There came a drought throughout the whole land. And lo and behold, the Brook Cherith dried up.

Then God told Elijah, "Go and live in the village of Zarephath, near the city of Sidon. There is a woman there, a widow woman, and she'll take you in, and I'll give her instructions to feed you."

Elijah did just as God told him. He went to this woman of Zarephath. And there God performed a miracle. As the Bible tells us, God multiplied her flour and oil so that it never ran dry all the time during that drought.

God provided for him. He took care of him through this woman. And when the woman's son died, Elijah raised him from the dead—brought him back to life.

For three years and six months now, there was no rain throughout all the land—no rain, no dew, nothing. The famine had moved across the land, and Ahab was as angry as he could be. He remembered what Elijah had said: "I'm going to call a drought, and you'll get no rain anymore till I tell it to rain."

Ahab was so mad. He put out word to find Elijah and kill him. He said, "If I don't do anything else in my life, I'll get Elijah and I'll kill him." And so he searched for the prophet—but God instructed Elijah to go to the king.

If I had been Elijah, and Ahab was out there with his army, wanting to kill me, and God was telling me to go look him up—I'd pray hard to see if I was listening to God correctly. But Elijah didn't hesitate a minute. Right away he went out and found the king.

When he found old Ahab, the king cried out, "So it's you, is it? The man who brought this disaster upon Israel!" But Elijah wasn't intimidated in the least.

Elijah thundered back and said (in 1 Kings 18:18), "You're talking about yourself. Your family refused to obey the Lord. Disaster is here because you worship Baal, and you're paying for that."

This Elijah was fearless. He wasn't scared of the king or anybody else. He challenged the king: "Now, I'll tell you what to do. Bring the people of Israel to Mount Carmel, and bring all the prophets of Baal, 450 of them, and bring the 400 prophets of Asherah—850 altogether." And Elijah said,

"Come on the appointed day and bring those 850 prophets. They can build an altar, and I'll build an altar, and we'll pray to our gods to send fire. Your prophets can pray to their god for fire, and I'll pray for my God to send fire. The one who sends fire, let him be God!"

Ahab agreed, and so the prophets came. On that day, you can just see Elijah, looking wild with his shaggy hair and sheepskin cloak tied with a piece of rawhide. And against him were the 850 prophets of Baal and Asherah. They were fixed up with their robes and their gowns and their ornaments and their vestments and their ties, and God only knows what all they were wearing. They were all fixed up, and here was the old rugged man standing there by himself, with only his servants with him.

The prophets of Baal prayed for fire all day to come down on their altar. They prayed all day long. They threw themselves on the altar, they cut themselves with knives until the blood gushed out. They cried to their god all the day long, but nothing happened.

Old Elijah started making fun of them. He said, "Maybe your god is out courting some woman. You better pray louder." They cried out louder and louder. Just imagine the commotion. But there was no answer from their god, and no fire for their offering.

Toward the end of the day, Elijah stepped up and called the people. He said, "Come over here." And all the crowd came over to Elijah. He built an altar and placed a young bull upon it, and he prayed. Listen to him pray: "O Lord God of Abraham, Isaac, and Israel, prove today that you're the God of Israel, and that I am your servant. Prove that I've done all this in your command. O Lord, answer me. Answer me, so these people know there's one God and one God alone." Just a short, beautiful prayer.

And look what happened! Fire flashed from heaven and consumed the sacrifice. And we read that when the people saw it, they fell to their faces upon the ground shouting, "Jehovah is God, Jehovah is God." Elijah had them kill the false prophets of Baal. And the rain came down on the parched earth and gave water to the earth.

Elijah was elated at the results, and I'm sure he thought in his heart, "Oh, this is glorious. There can be no question, now all of the nation will turn back to God. And Ahab will turn back to God, and Jezebel will turn back to God, and she'll see that there's a God in heaven." Elijah was thrilled.

But lo and behold, old Jezebel just turned the other way. You see, you can do that when you face God. When you face Jesus, you can come closer to him, or you can go farther from him, but you'll never be the same again.

You might be facing Jesus today, and you'll never be the same again. You'll come to Jesus and receive him, or you'll turn him away, but you'll never be the same.

Jezebel never turned to God. She became angry, and she said to Elijah, "You killed my prophets. I'm going to tell you something, Elijah; before this time tomorrow, you'll be dead." That's the repentance she had. And it was too much for Elijah. He just gave up. Here was this wicked queen, as unrepentant as ever, and Elijah retreated to the wilderness. He just went and left the whole thing, and departed to the wilderness.

That's where he felt at home. He was a man of the wilderness. He went back into the wilderness where he was most comfortable, and he sat in exhaustion under a juniper tree, and he wished to God that he could die. God bless him. He wanted to die, and then he laid down and went to sleep.

Pretty soon, an angel woke him up, and there was food miraculously furnished for him, and he ate and he slept. And in the strength of that one meal, he walked. He went forty days and nights until he came to Mount

Horeb, and there he stayed in a cave. God came and talked to him there, and appeared to him and recommissioned him. He told him, "Elijah, your work isn't done yet."

So Elijah found Elisha, a young prophet. Elisha wanted to follow Elijah. He wanted to be a prophet of God also, and so the two men traveled together. And the two of them, Elijah and Elisha, passed from the scene for about six years. And then upon his return, Elijah performed miracles for Jehovah, and he was always rejoicing and happy in God.

And then finally came the departure of Elijah.

This is what the Bible says: "And it came to pass, as they still went on and talked, that behold, there appeared a chariot of fire and horses of fire, and parted them both asunder, and Elijah went up by a whirlwind into heaven" (2 Kings 2:11).

And there you have the life of a great and mighty Elijah, and we'll not forget about him soon.

If Elijah was here today, I think he would tell us three things. I think this great man would first tell us, "Friends, sometimes you have to stand alone for God." In many ways, Elijah was a lonely man. He had no wife, he had no family, he had no associates, he had no one close to him. He had no close friends that we know of, except Elisha at the close of his life. And then he had a servant from time to time. But otherwise, he was a lonely man, all by himself. He came on the scene all alone, and he went to Ahab all alone.

And although he was alone, he wasn't afraid to stand before the wicked King Ahab. He delivered God's message, and there was no one beside him, and he fiercely made his stand for God. On Mount Carmel, the same thing was true: Elijah was all alone standing for God, calling people to repentance, to turn to Jehovah. He was alone on Mount Carmel with 850 prophets of Baal and Asherah to oppose him. Over against them all was one single individual, Elijah.

Elijah is an example for all of us. He stood against the wicked king and organized religion and all of the rest of it. He stood for God. I'm going to tell you, dear friend, there's a time when we need to stand for God. It will never be easy, but take your stand for God.

Elijah chose God, and he chose loneliness. He chose suffering. He chose immortality too, because he will live forever. That's the call for us to follow Jesus. I think of the persecuted church. More Christians are being put to death now than in any century since Christianity was established. Some of them are standing alone, but they're faithful to God. They sacrifice for God, and they're self-denying.

When Jesus says, "Take up your cross and follow me," that cross stands for death and self-denial. First of all, we deny ourselves, we die to ourselves, we live for Christ. But sometimes you have to do it all alone. And we read of these people in the persecuted church standing for Jesus all alone.

The second thing Elijah would tell us is this: no one is immune from depression. If mighty men of God like Elijah and John the Baptist can become discouraged, then we're not immune either.

Elijah had a tremendous victory. Elijah went to the servant at Beersheba, then he left his servant and went to Zarephath, and he went through all these things, but he faced them all and he thought at first, "Oh, surely this will win." But it didn't win, it turned against him.

How could such a thing happen? Well, there could have been several reasons. It could've been bitter disappointment after that tremendous victory on Mount Carmel, in such a terrible turnaround. Maybe a bitter disappointment makes us despondent or discouraged, and we believe it's too much, and we won't make it.

Or maybe we're physically exhausted. Maybe Elijah was just tired out to death. And that's why we need to watch our physical health, because there's a tie between the physical and the spiritual. Maybe I need to go to a doctor and get some help.

Or maybe it was loneliness. Elijah, when he talked to God, said this: "Even I only am left, and they seek my life to destroy it." He didn't know about those seven thousand believers who hadn't bent their knee. As I heard one pastor say one time, there were seven thousand believers in Israel, but it took God to find them. Where were they? Elijah didn't know them, but then he'd been in the wilderness. Maybe that was part of the reason.

For some reason, Elijah felt all alone and he felt discouraged. I think of shut-ins, and I think of people on sick beds, and I think of people who can't get out anymore. And you're alone, and you may get discouraged, and you think that nobody knows and nobody cares. And it may look like that, but don't ever forget that the Lord has said he will never leave us or forsake us, and you are never alone.

So this man, God deals with him. God gives him something to eat, and he gives him some rest. He lets the prophet know that he is near, and he cheers him up. He assures him of his success. He tells him, "I have work for you to do; there's a reason you are here." Some people will say, "Oh, I don't know why I'm here. I don't know why I'm living anymore." It's because God has work for you to do!

Then the third thing Elijah would tell us is that God always has his faithful remnant. He always has his faithful servants. Elijah thought he was the only one in the kingdom, but there were seven thousand others.

God will always have his witness. The day comes when we see this persecution of the church, and we see how they suffer, and we see how the devil wins in so many ways, and we see the wickedness in our own United States of America, and in all the other nations—they all have their certain sins.

It just seems like sin is in the saddle and is winning the day, and there's no end to it. But I'm going to tell you, God will always have his people. The day will never come when he won't have his people.

The devil can attack the church all he wants, but the gates of hell will never prevail against it. The church will always stand. And at the end, it will be victorious! The kingdoms of this world will become the kingdoms of our Lord and of his Christ, and the government will be upon the shoulders of Jesus Christ. And we will rule and reign with him. Don't you forget it!

So take heart. Elijah is telling us to just remember that God is alive, he is true, he is strong, he's going to have the last word. Greater is he that is in you than he that is in the world. That Holy Spirit who dwells in the believer is greater than all.

So the question is: Where do you stand with Jesus? Do you stand with the prophets of Baal, or do you stand with Elijah? You can't be in both camps. You have to be in one or the other. You'll either love God, or you love the world. You can't love mammon and love Christ at the same time.

I'm begging you today, open your heart to Jesus. If you've never done that, call upon the name of the Lord, and you will be saved. For as many as received him, to them he gave power to become the children of God.

You're not a child of God until you receive Jesus. As many has received him, they have power to become something they weren't—they become the children of God. As many has received him, to them he gave them power to become the children of God, even to them, to believe on his name.

In John 5:24, Jesus says, "Verily, verily, I say unto you, he that heareth my word, and believeth on him that sent me, hath everlasting life, and shall not come into condemnation." You won't go to hell, but will pass from death to life.

Dear heavenly Father, we thank you for Elijah, and we thank you for this great challenge, that he was willing to stand alone against 850 false prophets to show the whole nation of Israel that there is one God, the Lord God Jehovah, the God of Abraham, Isaac, and Jacob. And that he showed this by bringing down the fire, and that all false prophets couldn't get a spark.

Elijah proved beyond a doubt that you are God. And so, we're praying today, Lord, that people everywhere will see that you are God, the one true God, and that Jesus Christ is your Son, the great Savior of all, and that we need Jesus to get to heaven. He is the way, the truth, and the life. And so, may multitudes come to you today.

And Lord, we're praying also for the shut-ins and the lonely and the weary and those who are hurting. We're praying for the young people who may be caught up in some addiction, with all the drug traffic and all the horrible things happening, and they're in despair.

Help them to see that there's a God who will deliver them, a God who loves them, who will forgive them all their sins, who will come into their heart and dwell in their heart forever and take them eventually to heaven and make life worth living. Bless your people wherever they are.

And we'll give you the thanks and praise in Jesus' name. Amen.

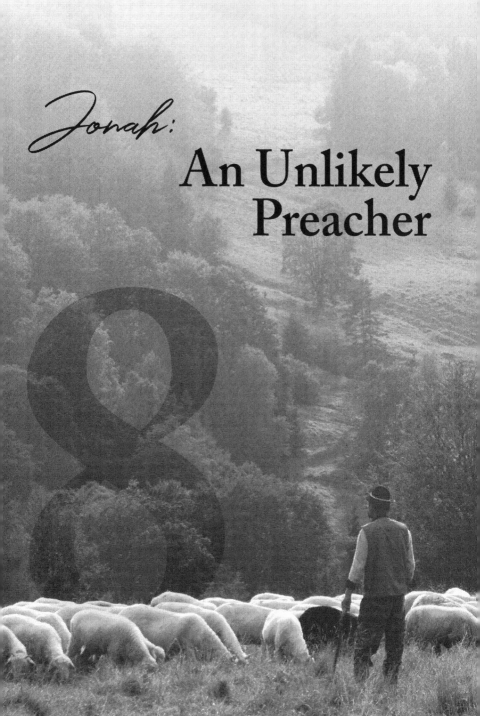

Jonah:
An Unlikely Preacher

8

Jonah:
An Unlikely Preacher
Jonah 2:1-10

[1] Then Jonah prayed unto the Lord his God out of the fish's belly,

[2] And said, I cried by reason of mine affliction unto the Lord, and he heard me; out of the belly of hell cried I, and thou heardest my voice.

[3] For thou hadst cast me into the deep, in the midst of the seas; and the floods compassed me about: all thy billows and thy waves passed over me.

[4] Then I said, I am cast out of thy sight; yet I will look again toward thy holy temple.

[5] The waters compassed me about, even to the soul: the depth closed me round about, the weeds were wrapped about my head.

[6] I went down to the bottoms of the mountains; the earth with her bars was about me for ever: yet hast thou brought up my life from corruption, O. Lord my God.

[7] When my soul fainted within me I remembered the Lord: and my prayer came in unto thee, into thine holy temple.

[8] They that observe lying vanities forsake their own mercy.

[9] But I will sacrifice unto thee with the voice of thanksgiving; I will pay that that I have vowed. Salvation is of the Lord.

[10] And the Lord spake unto the fish, and it vomited out Jonah upon the dry land.

Today we're thinking about the work of God in the Old Testament through Jonah and the giant fish. I don't know how many times I've preached about this, in almost seventy-five years now. It's just a joy to my heart, because there are so many good lessons in it.

When we talk about Jonah and the giant fish, the fish often takes center stage. But that is not the way it should be, because Jonah is the center of attention, and Jonah is the one we're going to look at.

Jonah was a Jew, and God told him to go to the Gentile city of Nineveh and preach so that the people might be saved. Now the Jew and the Gentile had nothing to do with each other, except that they hated each other.

That's the miracle of the church—because in the New Testament, through Jesus, the Jew and the Gentile hold hands and they love each other. But not in the Old Testament.

So we have a problem. Jonah hated the Gentile city of Nineveh with a purple passion. He didn't want to go and preach to them because, heaven forbid, they might repent and turn to God and be spared. And he didn't want them to be spared! He wanted them to go to hell, and the sooner the better. That's exactly how he felt.

Now here God was telling him: "I want you to go to Nineveh, and I want you to preach the wonderful word of God to these people." And God knew what Jonah was thinking.

Well, instead of going to Nineveh, Jonah went the exact opposite direction. Good old Jonah, just like a lot of us. I don't know what I would've done in his situation; I probably would have run away just as fast as Jonah did.

Instead of going east to Nineveh, Jonah decided to head west for Tarshish. And so he went to the port of Joppa and got on board a ship. He wasn't going to Nineveh. He had his ticket for Tarshish.

The Bible says that he went out from the presence of the Lord. Now that doesn't mean that God didn't know where he was, because the story is filled with God talking with him. God knew where Jonah was all the time. But when it says that Jonah went out from the presence of the Lord, it means that he went out of God's will.

He was defying God, and he turned his back on God, and went his own way. He got on this ship, and he headed west. And I can tell you this, friend: you can always run away from God, but you can't run far, because eventually you're going to run into him, sure as the world.

Before long, the ship found itself in a violent storm. The sailors on the ship were Gentiles, and they realized that somebody wicked must be on that ship, and that's why they were having trouble. So they cast lots to see who was causing the trouble.

Sure enough, it fell on Jonah.

He was probably somewhere sleeping—hiding from God and everyone else. The lot fell on Jonah, and so what should they do? There was only one thing to do: throw Jonah overboard. So they heaved him overboard.

But God had a big old fish there.

Now I don't know if it was a fish or a sea monster, and it doesn't make a bit of difference. Jonah was cast overboard, and wouldn't you know it, a giant fish was there waiting, and he was hungry, and his mouth was open—just at the exact time.

With one big gulp, Jonah was taken in, and he was inside that sea monster for three days and three nights. Then God intervened again, because Jonah prayed. Jonah was sick of the fish, and the fish was sick of him. The fish couldn't digest Jonah, and Jonah had learned a lesson.

He was going to listen to God from now on.

And so we read that the word of the Lord came unto Jonah the second time. What did God say the second time? He said the same thing he said the first time: "Arise. Go on to Nineveh, that great city. Preach unto it the preaching that I bid thee."

Jonah had learned a lesson. He did what God told him to do, and went to Nineveh. And so Jonah preached for three days. He stood on the street corners and preached the message of judgment from God. For three days he preached to a populace that included 120,000 children who didn't know their right hand from their left hand. That is, they didn't know anything about God. They didn't know anything about Jehovah—they knew only their false God. And Jonah preached.

And wouldn't you know it, the king heard the message, and he repented. And the king of Nineveh covered himself with sackcloth and sat on an ash pile, and the king sent word throughout the kingdom: "Repent and fast and turn to God." And God heard, and he spared Nineveh, that great wicked city, by the grace of God.

Now that's the story of Jonah and the giant fish. What lessons does this teach us? It teaches a lot of things.

It teaches us first of all that God has a plan for every one of us. It's a two-part plan. The first part of the plan is that we come to the Lord Jesus Christ and be saved. That's the first step. We're all sinners. There's none righteous, no, not one. The soul that sinneth, it shall die—that is, go to hell. If you die in your sins, you're going into hell. That's what Jesus said. And I'm glad to repeat it because that's what my master taught me to preach.

There's a heaven to gain and a hell to shun, and if we die in our sins, we're going to go into hell. But the Bible tells us also, "God is not willing that any should perish, but that all should come to repentance." He wants us to come to him, but if we refuse, then we take our place where the worm dieth not, and the fire is not quenched.

I wonder: Have you made that first choice? Have you accepted Jesus? That's the first part of his plan.

Now after we are saved, then God has a special plan of something for us to do as believers, as followers. It's a detailed plan for God, and you are important. It doesn't matter who you are. It doesn't matter if you have a seminary education or if you can't even read. God has a plan for your life, if you've accepted him.

God had a plan for Jonah, and Jonah was to preach repentance and revival. God had a plan for me, and I stumbled around a lot, but I think it was preaching, and that's what I do.

And Jonah at first didn't obey God's plan for him, though he knew what it was. I'm going to tell you, friend, you can disobey God if you want to. God has made us to be free moral agents. You don't have to receive Jesus. You can reject Jesus. You can take the Lord's name in vain. You can do that if you want to. You can trample underfoot the precious blood of Christ. You can refuse to do his will. He will respect your will.

So Jonah refused to obey God. That was his problem. And we read that he went out from the presence of the Lord. He left God's plan for his life.

Jonah didn't want to obey God. He wanted to go west instead of east. He didn't want to go to this place called Nineveh with these Gentiles.

And I want to tell you, you can obey God or you can disobey God. You can do as you choose. You have that choice, and Jonah sure chose wrong here. If you want to disobey God, Satan will be your friend, and he'll help you. Satan will have a boat for you. He had a boat for Jonah. He'll help you find a way out with great pleasure.

If you don't want to go to church, Satan will help you get an excuse for not going. He'll give you an excuse.

If you don't want to give God a tithe, he'll help you think of it in the wrong way. He'll say, "Oh, it's legalistic, it's Old Testament, it's for the Jew. It isn't for the Gentiles and doesn't apply today."

If you want to go out of God's will, Satan is going to help you every time! If you don't want to live the separated life, Satan will help you. He'll make you think evil is good and good is evil. If you want to disobey God, he'll have a boat for you. Count on it!

So be careful. God has a plan for you. Don't miss it. Don't take the wrong boat.

And then the second lesson is that God has all power. Some people have a problem with Jonah and the giant fish. By the way, the word is *costas*, which means a giant sea monster. We're told that God "prepared a fish," so it was a special creation that God made to swallow Jonah. So don't choke on that fact. Don't ever put a limitation on God's power. God created the whole universe out of nothing, by just his own word. He makes something out of nothing.

If you want to believe in evolution, there's nothing to back it up, and it is not a science, so don't limit God because of evolution. Evolution can't determine where you got substance, or where you got a mind, an intellect.

And so, like Jonah, if you don't want to follow God, the devil will help you. He'll take care of it.

Don't try to explain the miracles of God. God has the power to do it. No question about it.

116

Jonah was three days and three nights in the belly of that giant fish, and the only question I have about it is whether Jonah was dead or alive for those three days and three nights. He could have been dead. You know, I have a feeling that Jonah died in that giant fish, and when it vomited him up, God resurrected his life and gave him new life.

Remember what Jesus said in Matthew 12:40? "For as Jonah was three days and three nights in the whale's belly, so shall the Son of man, three days and three nights in the heart of the earth." Jesus was three days in the heart of the earth. He was dead, and then he was raised again! If God can do that for Jesus, he can do that for anybody.

Look at Lazarus, for instance, who was dead four days in the tomb. God raised him. It was no problem for God.

But it really doesn't matter if Jonah was alive for all that time inside the great fish, or if he was dead. It doesn't matter. Either way, it's a miracle. If Jonah stayed alive, it's a miracle. If Jonah was raised from the dead, it's a miracle. Never underestimate the power of God Almighty.

And then the third lesson from this is that God is a God of the second chance. I love to preach the wonderful word of God—it's the gospel of the second chance.

Look here at the mercy and grace of God. We see it when we see the word of the Lord coming unto Jonah the second time. That's grace.

You can look at all the religions of the world, and there is only one that has grace, and that's Christianity—Jesus. None of the other religions even know what you're talking about when you explain true grace, and half of these people who are Christians don't know what you're talking about either.

God's grace is greater than all our sin. Where sin abounded, grace did much more abound. "My grace is sufficient for thee," God says, and that wonderful grace gives us a second chance.

You have a second chance. God is always doing that. Look at David. He sinned terribly. But David repented, and God gave him a second chance.

Look at Peter, how he swore up and down that he didn't even know Jesus. He swore and he cursed, and yet, he repented through bitter tears. And God gave him a second chance.

God raised Jesus, who recommissioned Peter and said to him, "Go feed my sheep." And Peter went and fed his sheep, until his persecutors put him to death on a cross—head downward, because he said he didn't want to be crucified the same way Jesus was, because he wasn't worthy of it.

That second chance—that's what I love to preach. God has given me a second chance a hundred thousand times.

How many times have I gone to him and said, "Dear Father in heaven, I confess my sins." And if we confess our sins, he is faithful and just to forgive us our sins and to cleanse us from all our unrighteousness. I have failed Jesus over and over and over, and I've used my second chance and my third chance and my hundredth and my thousandth—I wouldn't have any idea how many. But every time I go to him, he forgives me, and I go on my way rejoicing.

And that's why I just love to preach the wonderful gospel, because I can tell you it doesn't matter what you've done. People always like to say, "I sinned against the light. I knew it was wrong, and I did it anyway. It was ignorance. I could see, but I knew it was wrong." That doesn't make a bit of difference. God's grace is sufficient. He'll forgive you. He'll give you the second chance or the thousandth chance. He is not willing that any should perish.

Jonah doesn't want to go to Nineveh; he was dead set against it. And

God later asked him, "Should not I have pity on Nineveh?" He was saying, "Jonah, you don't have any pity at all. You just have hate in your heart. Shouldn't I, God Almighty, have pity on Nineveh?" Jonah didn't have any pity. He just had the opposite.

But God asks his prophet, "Should I not have pity? Just because you don't care, should I not care?" And God is telling him, "I *do* care, and you're going to go, and those people are going to repent, and they're going to turn to God."

And so today I will ask that question. I wonder if we really have that love for the lost, like Jesus did. We have to have that longing. Are we sometimes like Jonah? We think, "I don't care what happens to my neighbor. He lives like the dogs. He's no good. He'll get what he deserves." I'm going to tell you, friend, don't ever ask God to give you what you deserve.

I never pray for justice. I pray for mercy. Somehow we have to get that from Jesus.

God is so wonderful. He's leading, guiding and directing, and he's telling us to come to the Lord. He's saying, "I have a heart for you." God is not willing that any should perish, but that all should come. Are you having a part in bringing these people to Jesus?

And then, quickly, another lesson: God is always in control. This just jumps out of this story.

Jonah was running from the Lord. God sent a tempest and almost sank the ship. God controlled the casting of lots, which pointed to Jonah. Then God sent a giant fish and had that fish open its mouth at the right time and swallow Jonah, in God's precise timing.

The ship was in a storm, and in the middle of the storm, the sailors threw Jonah out, and the fish gulped him down. Talk about a hole in one! That's perfect timing. That's God Almighty! That's my God, and he's always in control.

And that wasn't the end of the story. For God told the fish, "I want you to go over there and toss that man right onto the shore toward Nineveh, so people can see him come out of the fish." And wouldn't Jonah have smelled like a fish when he came out? And I wonder if some of those gastric juices made him yellow. I don't know, but he came out of there looking like something, believe me. And God put him right on that shore, at the exact time, just as he would have it.

And then there's more to the story. God prepared a gourd tree to shelter Jonah, then God sent a special worm to kill it. He caused an east wind to come and overheat the prophet, to make him faint. All these things were from God. They're the voice of God.

Sometimes we wonder: Where is God? He is there all the time. And the question we have to ask is, "Do I know this God?"

Have you accepted his son Jesus as your Savior? If you haven't, you need to do so right away. Call on the name of the Lord. Jesus tells us in John 5:24, "Verily, verily, I say unto you, he that heareth my word, and believeth on him that sent me, hath everlasting life, and shall not come into condemnation; but is passed from death unto life." And now you've heard this word in the best way I could give it. And when you hear it and believe on him who sent it, then right at the moment you believe, you'll possess everlasting life. You're born again. And Jesus says that you shall not come into condemnation. That is, you won't go into hell, but you've passed from death to life.

You can pray this prayer: "Dear Jesus, I'm sorry for my sins. I ask you to take them away. Come into my heart. And dear Jesus, I'll forsake those sins, and I'll follow you the best I can. Thank you, Jesus." You won't be perfect, but you've got to strive toward it, and to follow Jesus the best you can, and to give him thanks.

Now, if you made that prayer, you're a child of God. Your name is written in the Lamb's Book of Life. You'll never die. You'll be with Jesus. He'll hold you in his hands forever.

I know all the multitudes are praying. If you get your Bible now, turn to the Gospel of John. Read the Gospel of John, and pray. And someday I'm going to see you in heaven, and I'm going to rejoice, because of this wonderful, wonderful day when you prayed, "Dear Jesus, please save me. Come into my heart and save me." And you're his child.

I did that eighty-seven years ago—and he's never left me, and never will.

So now I want to pray for you:

Dear heavenly Father, we just thank you for every person who has just prayed that prayer. Now bless them and help them, Lord. And I'm praying, dear Lord, that you'll help the sick and the lonely and the weary and the discouraged, and be with the young people as they face so many temptations. Help them to turn to Jesus to give them strength and help. And help the children to know that you care for them, and that they can come to you.

And we pray that in all things, you'll have your way, and you'll be pleased. We want to thank you in Jesus' name. Amen.

Daniel: Faithful in the Lion's Den

9

Daniel:
Faithful in the Lion's Den
Daniel 6:16-23

BEGINNING IN DANIEL 6:16, we find the incident of Daniel being cast into the den of lions. I know we've heard this story a hundred times, but it's always thrilling to hear again. I'm excited to preach it, and I know you'll be excited as you hear this story retold:

> ¹⁶ Then the king commanded, and they brought Daniel, and cast him into the den of lions. Now the king spake and said unto Daniel, Thy God whom thou servest continually, he will deliver thee.
>
> ¹⁷ And a stone was brought, and laid upon the mouth of the den; and the king sealed it with his own signet, and with the signet of his lords; that the purpose might not be changed concerning Daniel.
>
> ¹⁸ Then the king went to his palace, and passed the night fasting: neither were instruments of music brought before him: and his sleep went from him.
>
> ¹⁹ Then the king arose very early in the morning, and went in haste unto the den of lions.
>
> ²⁰ And when he came to the den, he cried with a lamentable voice unto Daniel: and the king spake and said to Daniel, O Daniel, servant of the living God, is thy God, whom thou servest continually, able to deliver thee from the lions?
>
> ²¹ Then said Daniel unto the king, O king, live for ever.
>
> ²² My God hath sent his angel, and hath shut the lions' mouths, that they have not hurt me: forasmuch as before him

innocency was found in me; and also before thee, O king, have I done no hurt.

²³ Then was the king exceedingly glad for him, and commanded that they should take Daniel up out of the den. So Daniel was taken up out of the den, and no manner of hurt was found upon him, because he believed in his God.

Daniel is one of the most fascinating stories of the Old Testament. The name Daniel means "God is my judge." Daniel lived all his life as though God was his judge. He was standing before a righteous judge, and he was living for this God, and he was careful in his living.

We know that Daniel was a sinner just like the rest of us, but in the Bible, there isn't anything recorded in his life that would be marked as a sin. But as I say, he was a sinner. He needed to be saved by grace. But he lived a meticulous life, and he lived it for the Lord.

We don't know anything about Daniel's family or about his early life, except that he was one of the young people taken captive when Nebuchadnezzar overran Israel and overran Jerusalem. This took place in the third year of the reign of Jehoiakim, king of Judah, in about 605 BC.

Not only did Nebuchadnezzar capture the land, but he took the sacred silver and gold vessels from God's temple, and he also took young men. The young men were from different parts of the city and the area, and Nebuchadnezzar took them with him to Babylon. He wanted to have them trained so they could be added to the government personnel, and he could put a different little slant onto their thinking. So these young men were called to live in a special way.

Nebuchadnezzar took the finest young men he could find—not just anybody, but the choicest young men. And from Jerusalem came four of these young men, who would be about thirteen to fifteen years of age, so far as we can tell. In Babylon, they were given new names. Daniel was given the name Belteshazzar (Daniel), and his three friends were given the names Shadrach, Meshach, and Abednego.

These young men were all without blemish. They were handsome. They were people of wisdom. They had knowledge. They understood science. Nebuchadnezzar chose the very best he could lay his hands on, and he took those men back to Babylon with him, and they were put under the watchful eye of a man named Ashpenaz, who was the master of the eunuchs.

These four Hebrew young men were taught the letters and language of the Chaldeans, and they are taught for a period of three long years, after which they were to stand before the king, and he would examine them. They were also to have the food and drink of the king. They were to eat like a king—the best that could be had.

But Daniel spoke to Ashpenaz and made a request. He said, "Could my young men and I just live on vegetables and drink water? We don't want all the fancy food of the king, and we don't want liquor and wine and all of the rest. We just want vegetables and water." Then Ashpenaz agreed, and that's what they did. And God bestowed on the young men knowledge and skill and wisdom and understanding.

God gave Daniel a special gift: the ability to understand and interpret dreams and visions. So Daniel was endowed especially with this blessing of God.

At the end of three years, these four Hebrew young men were superior to all the magicians and enchanters in the matter of wisdom and understanding. They were head and shoulders above anyone Nebuchadnezzar had in his kingdom.

Then it came about that Nebuchadnezzar had a dream. At the appointed time, Daniel interpreted the king's dream. He and his companion were loaded with gifts, and they were honored in every way, because no one except Daniel could understand that dream.

With a later ruler of Babylon, King Belshazzar, Daniel promptly interpreted writing that appeared miraculously on a wall, as we read in Daniel 5. He interpreted this supernatural writing, and its meaning was that God had numbered the days of the king's reign.

Daniel gave this interpretation to King Belshazzar: "God has numbered the days of your reign and brought it to an end. You have been weighed in the scales and found wanting. Your kingdom is divided and is given to the Medes and the Persians." That's what the writing was about.

That's what the dream was about. And as tough as it was and as hard as it was to hear, Belshazzar had Daniel clothed with purple, and put a gold chain around his neck, and he was made the third ruler in the whole kingdom. But Daniel's interpretation was correct because that very night, Belteshazzar, king of the Babylonians, was slain, and Darius the Mede took over the kingdom.

But Daniel was of such stature and influence and wisdom that Darius turned to him, and he wanted Daniel to help him in the kingdom. He gave him a high place in the kingdom.

Thus it was that godly Daniel served under three and possibly four rulers. He served under Nebuchadnezzar, he served under Belteshazzar, he served under Darius, and he might have even served under King Cyrus.

Daniel was brought into a high position and remained there. Under Nebuchadnezzar, he was chief of the wise men. He was at the gate of the king. He was governor over the whole province of Babylon. Under Belteshazzar, he was made the third ruler of the entire kingdom. Under Darius the Mede, he was made as one of three presidents of the kingdom, and Darius even toyed with the idea of having Daniel rule the entire kingdom.

Daniel was always so great and dependable and loyal, and everyone knew he was a man of integrity, and so he was elevated to a high position. But when that happened, he also gained enemies. People were jealous of him.

Under Darius the Mede, Daniel aroused the jealousy of the other leaders in the kingdom who weren't granted all these favors, and some were afraid that Daniel might be given all of the kingdom. They were jealous of him.

They had to do something to stop him, but what could they do? They had determined to bring him down, and there was only one way they could do it, because he was perfect in all his ways before the king. He served in such a way that they couldn't find fault with him—but they could find fault with one thing, and that was his worship of God.

So they made their plan. These enemies went to the king and they said, "Why don't you make a decree that if anybody asks anything of anyone except you in the next thirty days, they will be killed by the lions?" So the trap was set, because they knew that Daniel faithfully prayed to his God at an open window three times a day. He prayed in full view of anybody walking by. He was not ashamed of his God.

So as soon as Daniel prayed, his enemies went to the king and they said, "Daniel has broken your law. He must be put into the den of lions. You have to get rid of him."

Darius was sick to his stomach. He loved Daniel. He saw now that it was a trap by these jealous leaders, but Darius was helpless, because it was known throughout the whole world that the laws of the Medes and the Persians could never, ever be broken. He'd made his law, and now Daniel had to be cast into the den of lions.

So Daniel was cast into the lions' den, but all the lions had lockjaw, and all they could do was to let Daniel pet them; they couldn't harm him. God had sent an angel to close the mouths of the lions. Daniel was unhurt and untouched.

By the way, God didn't send a band of angels to take care of all these lions. One angel took care of them all. That gives you a little idea of the power and might of the angels of God. Those angels watch over us and over all the people of God all the time, and they were watching over Daniel.

And so early the next morning, the king came to check. He was overjoyed at Daniel's safety, and he had the wicked rulers cast into the same den with the same lions, but these men were torn to pieces and devoured by the lions.

Then the last recorded vision of Daniel occurred on the banks of the Tigris River in the third year of Cyrus. Daniel was an old man, well over eighty, possibly even in his nineties. But he was still serving God. He was standing in the court strong for God, and so this man closed out his life.

So ends the story of Daniel, and how he was so faithful in his youth, and how he made his stand. I want to mention four lessons we can take from the life of Daniel.

First is that Daniel was a man of integrity. That is, he always kept his word. He was as honest as the day is long. In private or in public, he was honest.

I read of a young Christian man who made his university's football team as a starting split end, and he continued walking before God, and he prayed, "Help me in the climax of the moment to be honest. I pray for honesty, that one mark of integrity. I want to be that, Lord. I'll work on it through all this season while I play on this team. I'll be honest, a man of integrity."

When the rival team came to play his team, and it was homecoming, and this young man ran his route. He went into the end zone, and the quarterback passed a sharp pass to him. He caught the ball, but it was low, and he trapped it—the ball hit the ground at the same time that he grabbed it. However, the referee shouted, "Touchdown!"

The fans were cheering and shouting, and he was the hero of the game. But this young man knew that he'd trapped the ball. He walked over to the referee and said, "Sir, I trapped the ball." The referee canceled the touchdown, and they lost the game.

Now that young man was standing all alone. His teammates were shouting, "What does it matter, man? You had it. The referee ruled for you." But the young man said, "I can't take the credit. I didn't catch the ball." And why did he do that? Because he was a young man with integrity. And that's what Daniel was.

Integrity makes us honest. It makes us honest before the whole world. Integrity makes us honest in the light and also in the dark, when nobody's looking. Daniel was a man of integrity.

The second thing I want you to notice is that Daniel was a man of prayer. Oh, how he went to God! Over and over, we see him praying. When he needed help, and when he didn't especially need help, it didn't matter to him. He went to God at all times. That was his practice. It didn't matter what the circumstances were. He went to that open window and he prayed toward Jerusalem, toward his God and toward his temple. And God blessed him. He was a man of prayer.

When Nebuchadnezzar had his dream, and the other wise men couldn't figure it out, what did Daniel do? He called on his companions to pray, and then he'd go and answer to the king. And Daniel prayed, and God answered that prayer. He stood before the king and he gave an interpretation of the vision. He was a man of prayer!

Oh, my friend, listen. Don't go to God just when you're in trouble. Oh, it's right to go to him at that time; if you get into trouble, you're foolish if you don't go to God. But also, when things are going right, and when things are going well, go to your God then and thank him and praise him, and lean on him, and give him the credit! Be a man of prayer.

Third, Daniel was true to God no matter what it might cost him. And it did cost him—plenty.

Darius did all he could to save Daniel from going into the lions' den, but he couldn't break the law of the Medes and the Persians. The law could not be broken. It could not be altered. It could not be changed in any way. It stood as is. And so, after much soul-searching as the day came to a close, Darius had to call Daniel and put him into that den of lions—starving lions. Because when they go to put somebody in the lions' den, they starved the lions ahead of time for this purpose.

But lo and behold, there came an angel of God. And the angel of God protected Daniel from the lions. And before that happened, Darius was praying. He was praying that Daniel's God would deliver him. Darius was beginning to see that maybe the god of the Babylonians isn't the true God; maybe the God of Israel was the true God. And he's praying to that true God.

God sent one angel to guard Daniel and minister to Daniel. He encouraged him, and he helped him. That's what happened.

Do you remember when Jesus was tempted? We read, "And the devil leaveth him and behold, angels came and ministered unto him." So now the angel comes to minister unto Daniel and keep him company—just as God would send an angel to minister to Jesus years later.

Ever wonder who the angel was? Well, this wonderful angel, it looked like the son of God. It might have even been the Son of God. But he was an angel who came with all power. This could've been the same as Jesus, in his preincarnate form; we don't know. We know that the angel was in the fiery furnace, God's angels have great power and might, and they care for the people of God.

I know that God is always with his people, and I know that God sends angels to carry out his purposes. Look at Psalm 34:7, where David says, "The angel of the Lord encampeth around them that fear him and delivereth them." And Psalm 91:11: "He shall give his angels charge over thee, to keep thee in all thy ways."

And let me tell you something, friend. God doesn't always deliver us from the lions. You see that in Hebrews 11:33: "Who through faith subdued kingdoms, wrought righteousness, obtained promises, stopped the mouths of lions," but then verse 37 of the same chapter talks about the same people and the same God and the same faith, and it reads, "And they were stoned, and they were sawed asunder, and they were tempted, and they were slain with the sword"—and that's the persecuted church.

Sometimes God takes us out of harm's way, and sometimes he doesn't. As we pray, "Thy will be done," and whatever God wants is what we want—and that's the way Daniel lived.

Finally, let me say this. Daniel served God in his old age. "The righteous will flourish like a palm tree," the psalmist says. "They will grow like a cedar of Lebanon, planted in the house of the Lord. They will flourish in the courts of our God. They will still bear fruit in old age. They will stay fresh and green, proclaiming the Lord is upright. He is my rock and he is my fortress" (Psalm 92:12-15)—and he is the one that I will serve all the days of my life.

But I'm going to tell you something, friends. You can't serve him if you don't know him. You can't have his strength unless you know him. How do you know him? You say, "Dear Jesus, I'm sorry for my sins, and I ask you to come into my heart and take away my sins, and I'll turn from them, and I'll serve you the best I can. And thank you, Jesus." I did that eighty-seven years ago, and Jesus came into my heart, and he's been there ever since, and he'll never leave me.

If you are in a bed of sickness, you can serve the Lord by praying, and you can talk to Jesus, and you can witness to other people about Jesus, and you can let them know about the Savior. Live for him as long as you can live. God has you here for a purpose, and it wasn't just to live for yourself. He never left us to live for ourselves, but we're to think about other people. Jesus came to seek and to save that which was lost. He came to give his life a ransom for many, and that's what we have to do. We have to be witnessing for the Lord.

I was reading about Fanny Crosby, who was blind; when she was eight years old, she wrote this poem:

> Oh, what a happy soul am I,
>
> although I cannot see.
>
> I am resolved that in this world,
>
> contented I will be.
>
> How many blessings I enjoy
>
> that other people don't.
>
> To weep inside because I'm blind,
>
> I cannot and I won't.

That's what we need to do, all of us.

So you accept Jesus. Maybe you've drifted away from the Lord. Maybe you're like the prodigal son, and you've gone off some place and lived a riotous life. You forgot about God. Come back to him—because I'll tell you what he'll do. The Father will have his arms wide open, and he'll take you in his arms, and he'll bless you, and he'll forgive you all your sins. He'll take you back.

You say, "Well, I sinned against the light. I knew it was wrong, and I did it anyway." It doesn't make a bit of difference. He says, "Come unto me, all ye that are heavy weighed, and I'll give you rest." He says, "If you call upon me, I'll give you eternal life."

Dear Lord, I'm thanking you and praising you for the people all over the world who are making that prayer, and you're answering every one. Lord, I'm praying today for those on beds of sickness, those who are shut in, and the aged, and who can't get around. We're praying for the young people, Lord. Oh, the temptations they have! And we pray for the precious children who will turn to Jesus and ask Jesus to come into their heart. When we make that prayer, the minute we make it, our sins are gone. Our name is written in the Lamb's Book of Life.

Thank you for this wonderful story of Daniel and how he would not turn from you. He would let his light shine, no matter what it cost, and he was condemned to death, but the angel came. One angel came and took care of all of those lions, and they couldn't open their mouths or touch him. Thank you that you're such a great and wonderful God and Lord. We thank you that we know we can always rely upon you. And sometimes, Lord, we may have to suffer for you, like the persecuted church.

In Jesus' name, amen.

Esther:
Beautiful Inside and Out

10

Esther:
Beautiful Inside and Out
Esther 4:10-17

WHAT WE READ IN ESTHER 4 is at a point in history when Ahasuerus, the king of Persia, had been drunk and had signed a decree that all the Jews in the empire were to be put to death. His queen, Esther, was urged to come before him, and she did come before him to plead the plight of the Jews.

¹⁰ Again Esther spake unto Hatach, and gave him commandment unto Mordecai;

¹¹ All the king's servants, and the people of the king's provinces, do know, that whosoever, whether man or women, shall come unto the king into the inner court, who is not called, there is one law of his to put him to death, except such to whom the king shall hold out the golden sceptre, that he may live: but I have not been called to come in unto the king these thirty days.

¹² And they told to Mordecai Esther's words.

¹³ Then Mordecai commanded to answer Esther, Think not with thyself that thou shalt escape in the king's house, more than all the Jews.

¹⁴ For if thou altogether holdest thy peace at this time, then shall there enlargement and deliverance arise to the Jews from another place; but thou and thy father's house shall be destroyed: and who knoweth whether thou art come to the kingdom for such a time as this?

[15] Then Esther bade them return Mordecai this answer,

[16] Go, gather together all the Jews that are present in Shushan, and fast ye for me, and neither eat nor drink three days, night or day: I also and my maidens will fast likewise; and so will I go in unto the king, which is not according to the law: and if I perish, I perish.

[17] So Mordecai went his way, and did according to all that Esther had commanded him.

This is the story of a very beautiful woman. Esther was very beautiful. As a matter of fact, this story involves two beautiful women. The first one was Vashti.

Vashti and Esther were both queens. And they were queens to the same king. Both women were not only beautiful to look at, they were also beautiful within. That's a combination that is very seldom found: beautiful outside and beautiful inside at the same time.

The story opens with a riotous banquet. It probably was the most notorious banquet of all time. It was probably the worst drunken gathering of all time. For one thing, it lasted 180 days—that's six months!

This drunken celebration was given by Ahasuerus, king of Persia. He's also known as Xerxes. He was the ruler of a far-flung empire with 127 provinces. Each province had its own nobles and officials. And of course, each province had its own military personnel.

At this point in time, Ahasuerus was going to have a celebration for all these provinces, for all the leaders and all the personnel. And so they had this drunken feast. Finally it came to the last seven days, the last week. Everything was at a full pitch after drinking and eating for all this time.

The banquet was almost over now, and the period of this orgy was about to end. And Ahasuerus was thinking to himself, "What can I do? I've got to think of something to really be the climax for this whole thing."

Into his alcohol-inflamed mind came an idea, and it was something that only a drunken man could dream of. Because it came right out of hell. He was going to do one of the most despicable things beyond imagination. And it would take a wine-filled drunken mind to think of it.

The queen came to his mind, the most beautiful woman in the whole empire, indeed in all the earth. And this woman was going to be brought in so that all of these men could look on her and lust for her. And they were all in a drunken mess anyway.

And so he said, "Bring in Queen Vashti. And I'm going to have her stand before all of the multitude and display her body. I'm going to have her dance before all of these drunken revelers." The king commanded. And we read, "He commanded to bring Queen Vashti before the king with her royal crown in order to display her body for the people and the princes, for she was beautiful." The word *crown* in Hebrew can be translated as turban.

This idiot was asking her to come and dance, wearing only a crown or a turban, and nothing else—to dance before this wicked bunch. It was as wicked, as I say, as hell itself.

Not only was Ahasuerus a drunkard, he was evil and he was degraded. It's interesting to notice that the writer gives the account very plainly. And he tells us that when the king was intoxicated with wine, he had this thought and brought in this poor woman. The king was "merry with wine" as the King James Version says; the New International Version has it, "high spirits from wine." The king made that wicked, foolish decision while he was drunk, that's what he did.

So the message was sent to Vashti. And Vashti said, "No."

Now, in those days, the king could put her to death for refusing his request. He could just say, "Take her life. Get rid of her. Wipe her out." And they would do that. It could mean her death in a moment's time. Now whether that happened or not, we don't know; we don't know what happened to Vashti.

But she refused his request. And so Vashti goes down in history not as a beautiful woman (though she was a beautiful woman), but as someone who stood for that which was right. She stood for that which was honorable. And that's what makes her really great.

The king banished Vashti. Now he needed another queen. And he wanted the most beautiful woman in all the empire. So the search went out, and there was one woman who stood above all the others in beauty. There was no match for her. Her name was Esther.

And who was this Esther who was now going to be the queen? She was Jewish. But the court didn't know this. They didn't realize that. Her name in Hebrew was Hadassah, which means myrtle. Her Persian name was Esther, which means a star. And she was going to shine.

She was a star in physical beauty. But she was also a star in the beauty of her soul. Esther was an orphan girl, and so she had been adopted by her cousin, whose name was Mordecai. He took care of her and watched over her.

Now Mordecai had a good position under the king. But there was another man who was even greater, and that was Haman, who was the prime minister for all the kingdom. He was a proud man, and he wanted everyone to bow down to him when he passed by. He wanted you to kiss his ring. He was a very vain man.

But there was one man who wouldn't bow his head to Haman. That man was Mordecai. So Haman hated Mordecai with all his soul, because Mordecai, a Jew, wouldn't bow his head down in Haman's presence.

So Haman made a plan to take care of Mordecai. This was his plan. He went to King Ahasuerus, and he told him that all the problems in his kingdom were caused by Jews, and that the king should issue a decree to kill all the Jews.

This would include Mordecai. Haman was going to kill every Jew in the empire just to get rid of Mordecai. That's just the kind of man Haman was. So he told the king, "If you kill all the Jews, then you're okay." Then Haman added, "Here stamp this." And with his signet ring, the king made his stamp and issued the decree. And the word went out that he was going to kill every Jew in the kingdom.

Now there were two problems here.

The first was that nobody knew that Esther was Jewish. That hadn't been revealed; it had been kept a secret from the court.

Second, no one—not even the queen—could enter the presence of the king to talk about this decree without being invited. This was because if somebody wanted to assassinate the king, they could just go in and assassinate him. So they couldn't get to the king without an appointment. If they did approach the king, and he raised his scepter, then he would accept them. But if he didn't raise the golden scepter, then the visitor would be put to death on the spot, without any trial or jury or anything. That's the way they ruled.

So Mordecai got the word, and he knew there was only one person who could talk to that king and obtain deliverance for the Jews. And that was Esther. Esther would have to talk to him. Esther was going to have to tell him what the danger was. But Esther knew that attempting to speak to the king could cost her life.

So Mordecai spoke to Esther and said, "If thou altogether holdest thy peace at this time, then shall their enlargement and deliverance arise in the Jews from another place. But thou and thy father's house shall be destroyed. And who knoweth if whether thou art come to the kingdom for such a time as this."

So what Mordecai is telling Esther is this: "You've got to influence that king. You've got to talk to the king. That decree has to be changed. And if not, then we're all going to die."

Now Esther was living a good life, and everybody loved her. She was just so happy. But now she had to go to the king, and she might be put to death. She hadn't seen him in thirty days, hadn't even talked to him. And so she prayed. She asked all the Jews in this whole area to fast and pray.

And then she said something that has echoed down the corridors of time until it's famous even to this day. Esther said, "So will I go in under the king, which is not according to the law. And if I perish, I perish."

So that's exactly what she did. She entered the throne room. And as she came in, the king raised the scepter. And that meant that any request she had would be answered. The king was accepting her, and anything she wanted in that kingdom, she was to tell him.

Esther didn't hesitate. She said, "Oh king, if it pleases the king, let my life be given me at my petition. And my people at my request. For I am sold, I and my people, to be slain and to be destroyed, and to perish."

The king was absolutely dumbfounded. His mouth dropped open. He had signed this decree in a drunken state. He didn't even know he had signed it and made the stamp.

The king said, "Where is he? Who is he? Where is he who would presume in his heart to do such a thing?" And Esther, a beautiful queen, the queen of the empire, said, "The adversary and enemy is this wicked Haman." When the king heard that, he said immediately, "Go and destroy that man as quickly as you can."

Esther is known for her beauty, but she was more than beautiful outside. She was beautiful inside. And it's a beautiful story of how she was willing to lay down her life for her people, for a cause that is right. And she won the day, and the people were spared. It's a beautiful, beautiful story.

Now what do we take from the story?

The first thing that stands out—just as big as a house—is to lay off the liquor. In this story, a beautiful woman, Vashti, was banished from her position as queen of the empire because a drunken man made an impossible demand. And a whole race of people are about to be exterminated because of a drunken king who made a law he didn't understand and didn't know about. He did it when he was drunk.

Christians ought to keep clear of this vice. Christians ought not to drink even in moderation. Christians ought to abstain from liquor in total abstinence altogether, and that includes beer. No good can come from liquor. How many a young man or young woman has given up their virtue because their reasoning ability was impaired while they were drunk or under the influence of liquor?

One of my best friends died from drinking. And he was drinking beer, that's all he ever drank, until he was bloated and poisoned and died.

I'm going to tell you this, too: some of my very best friends are alcoholics and have been alcoholics. And I love them just like I love anybody else. And they would say amen to my plea: Don't touch alcohol, and don't fool with it.

I want to warn young people especially. If you experiment with alcohol, you start down a road that can destroy your body and your soul unless you're careful. When you drink socially, you never get addicted, you're just a bad influence. Because every young person is going to do the same thing.

I knew one man who drank moderately all his life, and I never saw him drunk. "Well," you say, "that's the way I want to drink." But the next fellow can't do it. And he's caught up, and he's lost in some terrible sin. Take godly Esther as your example, not drunken Ahasuerus. Don't talk about moderation, talk about abstinence. And that goes for tobacco and drugs as well. Lay off of the liquor.

Then secondly, don't rule God out. When you read this intriguing story, you cannot help but see the hand of God. You cannot help but see the providence of God. You can't help but see how God deals with individuals and how he deals with whole nations. It doesn't matter to God whether it's one man or the whole world. God rules over them all. So don't rule God out.

The word *providence* is derived from a Latin word, *providio*. The prefix *pro* means "before"; the root *vidio* means "I see." And so what the providence of God simply means is that God sees events before they happen. He sees in the future as plain as day. God is never surprised. He sees it all; that's the providence of God.

So this wonderful God knows all things, he sees all things, he works out all things. He's invisible, yes, but he's there. He's in control of all things.

Some people worry about the book of Esther, and they say, "Well, the word *God* isn't mentioned in the whole book." That's right, it isn't. But he's there. You see the power of God there. You see the fact of God there. You see the wisdom of God there. You see the perfect timing of God there. Even an atheist couldn't help but see God in this book.

So look at this story. Look at it, and see how God is standing in the shadows, and he works out all things with his people.

The wonderful providence of God—rest upon that, lean upon that. When we see that providence, and we believe in the providence of God— that he sees all things and controls all things—it gives us faith. It gives us confidence. It gives us trust, and assurance, and joy, and peace. Because God has his hand at the helm, and he's the captain.

He's guiding this whole world, and he's in charge of it. It's not left to the whim of chance. It's not left to what happens, whichever way the wind blows. We're not here controlled by some quirk or by some strange things that happen to us. We're not left here to the winds that blow, or hanging on the roll of a dice. We're in the hands of a loving God who cares. And he provides for us and loves us and helps us when we trust him. Don't ever leave God out of your life. Don't leave God out of the picture as you think of your life.

That brings me to the third thing: God has a plan for your life. When Esther realized that God Almighty had a plan for her life, she began to act. And history was changed.

This woman Esther was enjoying great joy and happiness as a queen. She had everything at her disposal, and everybody loved her. She was beautiful, she was courageous, she was almost worshiped by the people. As a matter of fact, in Esther 2:15 we're told, "And Esther obtained favor in the sight of all them that looked upon her." She was a favorite of the king, which was no small matter.

But Mordecai reminded her: "Perhaps you have this position, perhaps you're the queen, perhaps God has given you all this for just such a time as this."

There was a crisis, and the Jewish nation was to be wiped out. And Mordecai was telling her, "Esther, just remember this: you can be the salvation of the Jewish race. And God has a plan to save the Jewish race, and you're the key. You're the one to do it."

When that thought sank into her mind and her heart, it changed Esther from a pleasure-seeking woman to a woman with purpose in life, a woman with a challenge in life, a woman who had a goal in life. It made Esther strong to know that God was counting on her to carry out his purpose and his plan.

So this beautiful woman said, "I will go in to the king. And if I perish, I perish."

That fact tells me that God has a purpose in my life, and he has a purpose in your life. It's a detailed plan, and life is a serious thing; life is an honest thing. Don't live as though it's something useless, or meaningless, or futile, or of no value. Don't look at it that way.

Maybe you feel useless in this life. Maybe you're a shut-in, maybe you're in advanced years, maybe you're bedridden. And you say, "I'm not worth anything. I'm too old. They don't have a place for me." That's America's ideas, friend; it isn't true in other countries where age is revered, but it is in America. There's such a thing as ageism. And I've experienced it, and it isn't nice.

But listen to me, my friend, no matter what your age or your condition. Maybe you can't even get your head off that pillow. But as long as you breathe, you're of great value to God Almighty. And as long as you live, God has a purpose for your life, and don't ever forget that. You are of great value to God. You are important, my friend. And when your work is done, he'll take you home. But if he hasn't taken you home, his plan isn't done with you yet. You are important.

Esther lived on a mundane level. But when she understood that God had a work for her to do, she stood tall and magnificent and beautiful. And she declared, "No matter what happens, if I perish, I perish. But I'm doing God's bidding. Let the chips fall where they may." And I might add, many a Christian has perished out in a foreign field who went there with God's plan. But his plan was to go and to sow the seed and to start the thing in motion.

Oh friend of mine, realize that you're called to a great destiny, to honor, to glory, and to immortality.

You make the first step by receiving Jesus Christ into your life, because you can never do it unless you have Jesus Christ in your heart and in your life, and unless he's on the throne in your life, and you're yielded to him. Esther was totally sold out to God, and you and I have to be sold out to Jesus Christ. You and I have to be just like Esther, and just be sold out to God. And look at what one person did. Esther saved an entire nation!

I read just the other day about what a difference one person can make. In 1776, one vote gave America the English language instead of German. In 1845, one vote brought Texas into the union. In 1868, one vote saved President Andrew Johnson from impeachment. In 1876, one vote gave Rutherford B. Hayes the United States presidency. And listen to this: one vote in 1923 gave Adolf Hitler control of the Nazi party.

Don't sit on your hands and say you don't count. And if you're a young person, know that your one voice could keep a whole group from going wrong; your one voice could take them to the wrong way or to the right way. You are important.

Esther is calling upon all of us, men and women, young and old, to stand up for the right even though it may endanger your life. God is counting on you, just as he did for Esther.

Make your stand for Christ. If you've never done that, accept Jesus Christ, give your life to Christ.

And if you have accepted the Lord, if you are a Christian, then surrender to the Lord, submit to the Lord. Make him first. Seek ye first the kingdom of God and his righteousness, and these other things will be added unto you.

I read a story from Walter Wangerin Jr., a famous story about his son Matthew, when Matthew was small. He says that Matthew was a headstrong little boy, and when he decided to do something, he didn't think about the consequences, but just did it. One day Wangerin went into Matthew's room and he found him sitting there on the bed with a stack of comic books. He asked where Matthew got them. Matthew said, "I got them from the library." And his father said, "You didn't check them out from the library; you stole them, didn't you?" And Matthew said, "Yes."

So the father marched Matthew back to the library with the comic books to apologize and restore what was stolen. The librarian gave Matthew a good lecture on how it was wrong to steal.

The following summer, they vacationed in Vermont and had a nice vacation. When they got home, Wangerin went into his son's room, and there he was with a stack of comic books. He'd stolen them in Vermont and brought them home with him. And Wangerin says, "I took those books and I started the fireplace. And I threw a comic book in there and I would say, 'Thou shalt not steal,' the seventh commandment. I took every book, I burned every one; 'Thou shalt not steal, thou shalt not steal.'"

But a year later, Matthew stole more comic books. This time his father felt he had to spank this boy. So he put him over his knee, and with his bare hand he hit him five times. "I wanted him to feel it," he says, "but I was so mad, I didn't want to hurt him. So I did it five times."

But Matthew wasn't crying. So his father stepped out of the room. And Wangerin says, "I broke down and I wept uncontrollably. I went to the bathroom and I washed up and cleaned up. Then I went back to my boy. And I had a talk with him."

Years later, when Matthew was a teenager, he was coming home with his mother one day after they'd been shopping. They were talking and reminiscing. And Matthew said to his mother, "You know, after that incident with dad, I really never stole anything again."

His mother said, "I suppose the reason was because your father spanked you."

"No," replied Matthew. "It was because when he stepped out of the room, I could hear him crying." That's what got to him.

We love Christ, and we don't want to hurt Christ. Do you remember when Jesus was here? And we're told, Luke says that he wept over the city of Jerusalem: "And when he was come near he beheld the city and he wept over it." A city that rejected him, that turned him away, that wouldn't listen to him. He wept over them, and he wept over their sins.

So we don't want to make Jesus weep. I don't want to make him weep. I don't want to turn him away. I want to know he loves me. And I'm serving him not because he's going to put me into hell if I don't. I serve him not because he may give me some disease or break my neck or something like that. I'm doing it because I love him. I love the Lord Jesus.

And so today, we want to give ourselves to Christ. And then as Christians, to submit totally to the Lord and walk with him.

Let's look to the Lord in prayer.

Dear heavenly Father, we thank you for this beautiful story of Esther. And that she was so totally given to you that she was willing to die for the cause that you called her to. We thank you for this story, and we pray that we'll draw strength from it so that we will trust you and lean upon you no matter what happens. No matter what the day may bring, we belong to you. And we will be servants of yours.

Bless your people wherever they are. You know, Lord, you're as close to them as you are to us. And we're all one body in Christ. And to those who don't know you, those who are unbelievers, those who are lost, help them to know that you want them to be a part of this body through coming to Jesus your Son. And whatever is done and said, may it all be to the glory of the wonderful, wonderful Lord Jesus Christ.

For we pray it in his name. Amen.

Jesus:
Our Born King

11

Jesus:
Our King Is Born

Matthew 2:1-12

WE'RE READING FROM MATTHEW 2, and this is when the magi come from somewhere in the East, and they come to Jerusalem, and then they go on to Bethlehem. This is the story.

¹ Now when Jesus was born in Bethlehem of Judaea in the days of Herod the king, behold, there came wise men from the east to Jerusalem,

² Saying, Where is he that is born King of the Jews? for we have seen his star in the east, and are come to worship him.

³ When Herod the king had heard these things, he was troubled, and all Jerusalem with him.

⁴ And when he had gathered all the chief priests and scribes of the people together, he demanded of them where Christ should be born.

⁵ And they said unto him, In Bethlehem of Judaea: for thus it is written by the prophet,

⁶ And thou Bethlehem, in the land of Juda, art not the least among the princes of Juda: for out of thee shall come a Governor, that shall rule my people Israel.

⁷ Then Herod, when he had privily called the wise men, enquired of them diligently what time the star appeared.

⁸ And he sent them to Bethlehem, and said, Go and search diligently for the young child; and when ye have found him, bring me word again, that I may come and worship him also.

⁹ When they had heard the king, they departed; and, lo, the star, which they saw in the east, went before them, till it came and stood over where the young child was.

¹⁰ When they saw the star, they rejoiced with exceeding great joy.

¹¹ And when they were come into the house, they saw the young child with Mary his mother, and fell down, and worshipped him: and when they had opened their treasures, they presented unto him gifts; gold, and frankincense and myrrh.

¹² And being warned of God in a dream that they should not return to Herod, they departed into their own country another way.

Christmas is my favorite time of the year. I have so many wonderful memories that take me back home, memories of home, with my mother, and with my brothers, and with my sister, and our school days, and our school programs, and our Sunday school in that little country school. I have a lot of wonderful memories.

Of course, Christmas Eve does have a little tinge of pain because it was on Christmas Eve in 2005 that my wife Beulah went to be with Jesus. When I come to Christmas, I rejoice and give praise. But always, in the back of my heart, I think about my wife and how she's safe at home. Christmas is a special time. It's a family time, and we always have so many good memories.

The coming of the Lord is so important. As a matter of fact, the coming of Jesus broke time in half and we have BC and we have AD, and that's when Jesus came. He was raised from the dead. He separated time, the way we keep time, and the atheists hate to put AD and they hate to put BC, because it testifies to the fact that Jesus came and was raised from the dead. They don't like it, but there isn't a thing they can do about it, except to fuss.

We're looking at the message of the star. Matthew tells us about the birth of Jesus and how there was then a celestial illumination, some brilliant, beautiful shining star. The whole world saw that star. They didn't know what it meant, but they saw it. That star shone about two thousand years ago, and everybody saw it. The shepherds, who were Jewish, saw it, and then the magicians or the magi, who were Gentiles, saw it. And you have seen it, and I have seen it, and millions have seen it, and it is God coming to help us.

Let's look first of all at the star as a sign. It was an emblem of a king. The sign was interpreted by the magi to be the mark of a king. We read that they inquired, "Where is he that is born King of the Jews? We have seen his star." It was Jesus' star, and they recognized it as that. We don't know where the magi came from. They were on a very hard part of the earth, but they saw that star, and they came to Jerusalem.

This is what they said: "Where is he that is born King of the Jews?" Do you see that? King of the Jews. They didn't say, "Born to become King of the Jews." They were saying, "He *is* the King of the Jews, right now as a baby." He is *born* King of the Jews, and they understood that. They were talking about this great and wonderful Jesus, this great and wonderful shepherd.

The sign was understood in previous days. We read about the Star out of Jacob, and Balaam had his prophecy, and he talked about the scepter of a king, and the Star out of Jacob in Numbers 24:17. In Revelation 22:16, Jesus was spoken of as the bright morning star. That star had significance, and it spoke of Jesus.

The star was a symbol that was easily seen. Everybody could see it because it was elevated and it was above all. It was conspicuous. It was seen about all parts of the world—that wonderful star shining.

Of all of the stars shining, there was one that had more splendor in beauty, and it stood out from the rest, and it's this wonderful star. That star means that there's a coming one who will rule and have influence over all the world, and that's exactly what happened when Jesus came.

The star indicated an extraordinary prince. It was more than the symbol of a man-made object. It was an extraordinary phenomenon. It meant that this wasn't just another prince born among men; this was a special prince, and it's a special star.

It was an unusual apparition in that it wasn't a fixed star, because it moved. It went before the magi and showed them the way. It was not a recognized planet, because it was too near the earth. It wasn't an ordinary meteor because it blazed too steadily. It was a supernatural star, and it was a token of a supernatural prince, Jesus Christ, the Son of God.

We don't know what the star was. It might have been a conjunction of stars clustered together or it might have been a special star that was just created by God, just like he created the special fish to swallow Jonah. It was that one star for that one occasion—that's what I think, but we'll find out when we meet the Lord.

In this heavenly brilliance, it spoke to the magi off in a foreign country, and they said, "This is special, this is the King of the Jews." They had heard somewhere, they knew somehow in their studies, and these men were more scientists than astrologers. They were men who were scientists and they studied the stars, and they studied the things of God, and they were looking for it, and here it came.

It was just the exact time for this to happen, because the Jewish nation was in decline. They were getting smaller, and they were having trouble, and it was time for this king to come and give them hope and encouragement. Daniel's weeks of prophecy were fast running to an end, and so the Son of God has to come, and so the star came. In Israel, they looked for their Messiah. In the Gentile nations, they had seen Jewish traditions about the coming of the Messiah.

But even among the Gentiles, there was also a suspicion. For instance, Cicero talks about this tradition of the coming of the Messiah. And the magi, who were familiar with Jewish prophecy, felt that the time was near.

The star came, and the star directed these people to Christ. It moved over the heavens until it came and stood over where the young child was. You'll notice that this was a house. He wasn't in the manger anymore. By this time the magi arrived, he might have been two or three years old. And the star was shining in brilliance that night, a special brilliance just for one reason, and that is to point to Jesus Christ, to direct people to Jesus Christ.

The angels that night sang over the Judean hills, and they did it for just one reason, to point and direct people to Jesus Christ. That was God's plan then, and that is God's plan now: that you and I are to direct people to Jesus Christ, whether you're a preacher or whether you're a Sunday school teacher, or whether you sing in the choir, or whatever you do. Whether you just live a normal little life, and you're not standing out in anything, but you are there to direct people to Jesus Christ.

At *The Christian Worship Hour*, that's all we have in mind: to point to Jesus Christ so that lost people dying in their sins and going to hell can find eternal life through Jesus. The suffering saints and the struggling people who need comfort, we're directing them to Jesus Christ. He is the answer. There is no other answer. Always remember: Jesus Christ is forever and always the culminating with God. At his birth, God pointed to Christ. At his baptism, God pointed to Christ. At the Mount of Transfiguration, God pointed to Christ.

Just remember this: God's heart is in his Son, and Christ is at the center in the circumference. He is the circumference. He is the A to the Z. He is the Alpha and the Omega. He is the first and the last. He's the beginning and the ending. Jesus Christ is all in all. If you want to have favor with God, my friend, if you want to get to the heart of God, you get to Jesus Christ and fall in love with Jesus Christ, because that's where the heart of God is centered. Honor his son. Love his son. Receive his son.

If you've never prayed that prayer, this is the prayer that I prayed when I was ten years old. I just told Jesus, "Dear Jesus, I'm a sinner, and I ask you to come into my heart and take away my sins." Jesus says, "I stand at the door and knock. If any man hear my voice and open the door, I will come in." You've got to open the door. How do you open the door? Just ask him to come into your heart. Maybe you'll feel happy, or maybe you'll feel sad, or maybe you won't feel anything. But just take God.

It's a transaction where you believe God and you accept his Son, and you ask him into your heart—and then you have eternal life. When you know the Lord, then you'll just be rejoicing and happy as you walk with Jesus Christ, the wonderful Savior.

Now, the stars have been used over the ages for guidance, and that's what this star was doing—guiding people, guiding the whole world to one spot. When Jesus said, "I am the way, the truth, and the life." There's only one way to God, and that's in his son, and that's the whole of what this star was pointing to.

I was reading about the stars and how the mariners of ancient times depended on them; before they had a compass, the only way they could sail the seven seas was by the stars. The star of Bethlehem was a guide, and so today Jesus Christ is the same thing, and he's calling people. He's a star that guides us and brings us to God. He's a star out of Jacob, we're told, this wonderful Lord Jesus Christ. And he said, "Follow me. Follow me." Put your faith in Jesus Christ and follow him.

Sometimes I hear people say, "If I had been one of those shepherds, I would've followed Jesus. I would have gone to Jesus. If I had been one of the magi, those wise men, I would have come all that distance." I want to ask you something: Are you following Jesus now? If you're not following Jesus now, you would not have gone to Jesus then.

Don't procrastinate. Just repent and confess your sins. If you've drifted away from the Lord, come back to him. Sometimes people say, "Well, I sinned, and it's a sin that God won't forgive, because I accepted Jesus, and then I knew I shouldn't do it, but I sinned anyway." Well, Jesus will receive you into heaven. The Father will receive you into heaven just like the man received the prodigal son. That's the story Jesus told, and he told that for the sake of the people who drift away and go into sin. The young man knew better, but he took his inheritance and he lived as recklessly as he could, and as wickedly as he could. I don't know what all he did; it's just as well we don't. But when he came to his senses, he was destitute, at his wit's end, and he was out in the pigpen eating the husks. He came to himself, the writer in Luke says, and the prodigal son said to himself, "My father has servants who are treated better than this; I'm going back to my father."

And in Luke 15:20 we read, "When he was yet a great way off, his father saw him and had compassion, and ran and fell on his neck, and he kissed him." That's what God will do if you will just come to Jesus and put your faith in him, and receive him. But you have to make that stand where you accept Jesus Christ as your own personal Savior.

I beg of you then to do this. Come to the Savior. And you know, we can drift away after we accept Jesus. We can drift away. We can get lukewarm, and we can get off course.

It reminds me of a story of a young sailor, and they were sailing by the stars, and the old captain took the boy and he said, "Now, you keep that star right at the mast. Keep that mast directed right at that star. I'm going to get some sleep, and if you have any trouble, you come and tell me." In the middle of the night, the boy came and woke the captain up. He said, "Sir, I passed that star; what do I do now?" He was off course.

And there are people who get off course; it's easy to get off course, because the devil tries to do that to us. He does everything he can to get you to drift away from the Lord. He doesn't want you to accept Christ in the first place, and then when we do accept Christ, he'll do everything he can to get us off course, to get into this or that, it doesn't have to be a sin. It can be maybe golfing, or something like that. You skip church to go golfing, hunting, snowmobiling, whatever it is; the Lord only knows. Something else gets put in the place of Jesus in your life, and so you need to hear what the old captain says: "Get back on course." You get lined up with that star, get lined up with Jesus. Accept him, and then if you have drifted, just ask him to forgive you. Come back to Jesus.

I want you to notice something, too, dear friend: there's a star in every sky. I believe with all my heart that there's a star in every sky, wherever you live in this world, I don't care where you are. If you, in your heart, will search with your whole heart to find God, if you honestly seek to find

God, if your heart is really truly hungry, then I believe with all my heart and soul that God's going to put a star in your sky.

You can come to him if you're really sincere. As I said, these wise men lived in a very remote land. They were actually out of touch with the rest of the world. There was a man, Marco Polo, and in spite of the most painstaking inquiries and searches, he just couldn't exactly find where these men came from.

When that star came into their sky, they were obedient to it, and they traveled miles upon miles, because they were coming to the Lord Jesus. To the wise men, the astronomers, God speaks to them in the star in a heavenly body. To the shepherds watching their flocks by night, he fills the sky with angelic angels. To the fishermen, Jesus talks about becoming a fisher of men. To the woman at the well who's drawing water, he talks about the living water that he gives, so that we'll never thirst.

In every sky, Jesus has a star. If you look for it, you can find the Savior. Open your eyes. Open your heart. Open your soul. Let the light of God blaze in, because God says, "Whosoever will, may come." You can come to Jesus.

Now, it may cost a price to come to Jesus. These magi had to travel all those miles. They never faltered. The last star led, and they followed. They were prepared to pay any price to find the Savior, to find the King of the Jews. They didn't care what it cost. These men were traveling, and there was absolutely nothing that could keep them from the truth. And when they finally found the Christ child, they fell down before him. These great scientists and wise men of the East fell down and they worshiped the Son of God.

They had an honest search in their heart, and they would never settle until they got there, and that's exactly what they did. They came and they opened up their gold and their frankincense and their myrrh. These were all costly gifts. So they had come to worship this wonderful Lord Jesus Christ. They didn't bring him gifts from a rummage sale, or something they took out of their closet, and put it out as a sacrifice to Jesus. But they brought gold and frankincense and myrrh.

Mary and Joseph were as poor as church mice. It wasn't long before Herod would make an awful decree, and they would have to escape and take Jesus into Egypt. How were they going to travel into Egypt? They didn't have a nickel to their name. But now they had gold and myrrh and frankincense. You could sell any of it, you could use any of it. See how God provides? "I want you to take my Son into Egypt, and here's the money to take him with. Here's your credit card. Take him into Egypt."

There was something here we don't want to miss, and that's old Herod. Herod was a cruel man. He was a wicked man. He was a murderer. He ordered the deaths of his own wife and her two brothers because he suspected them of treason. He was married at least nine times, and he had two of his sons put to death. He was an evil man.

Now, when he heard that somebody was born who was King of the Jews, he thought, "I got to get rid of him." A demon stirred up within him when he thought of another who might take his place. He was a troubled man, and he ordered that all the babies there in Bethlehem be killed, because he suspected that one might be the king. He might have trouble with him; he might try to steal his kingdom.

But Jesus came for a different kingdom, a kingdom that's righteous and pure and holy, the kingdom of God. He didn't want Herod's lousy kingdom.

We're told that Herod was so wicked that he gathered a huge number of Jews, and ordered that when he died, all that multitude would be killed, so that all throughout the land they would mourn his death. There would be weeping. That's the kind of a man he was.

When this wonderful Lord Jesus Christ came, it caused a lot of grief, because Satan was there, and Satan is going to oppose God's kingdom every step of the way, as long as he can. This wonderful thing we see is this wonderful star, and we see it as a marker that this is the king. We see it as a guide to bring the people to the house where they can worship him, and then he guides us. This wonderful Lord Jesus Christ watches over us and helps us.

William Barclay says, "The magi were good and holy men who sought for truth"; and he says, "It was their profession to watch the heavens, and some heavenly brilliance spoke to them of the entry of a king into the world."[6] The star was their sign and signal for going to Jerusalem. God does that today; he guides and directs us, and we come to worship him. We worship the Lord Jesus Christ, we come, and we bring our gifts, just like these wise men brought their gifts.

But before we give any money, we give ourselves, because God has all the money in the world, and he wants us to give ourselves to him. He wants to be first. He says, "Seek ye first the kingdom of God and his righteousness." So put Christ first, put Jesus first, and then you can give your gold and your frankincense and your myrrh, and you can give your talents and your time, and give all that you have—and you'll be a witness for the Lord. But first you've got to give yourself. "Seek ye first the kingdom of God, and his righteousness, then all of these things will be added unto you."

The wise men heard about him, and they knew about him, but they wanted to see him. They studied about him, they heard about him, but that wasn't enough; they wanted to know him. The angels sang, and then all of a sudden, the shepherds knew about Jesus being born in Bethlehem, but they wanted to see and know him. Not just know about him, they wanted to *know* him.

You must never be satisfied with knowing about Jesus Christ until you personally know him as your own. I beg of you today, be a follower of Jesus Christ. If you aren't, just say this prayer. Just say, "Dear Jesus, I'm a sinner." Ask him into your heart: "Come into my heart, dear Lord. Save me from my sin, and I'll turn to you. I'll follow you the best I can." Then you'll have eternal life, and you won't just know about him; you'll *know* him, and then you walk with him.

I've been with the Lord eighty-seven years. I've had my ups and downs spiritually. I haven't always been on the track, but our God has always drawn me back. I can just trust Jesus and love Jesus, and I know someday I'm going to see him face to face.

That's the relationship we can have with him. Just remember this: everything points to Jesus in this world. Do as the wise men. Do as the shepherds. Do as the apostles. Do as millions and millions of people have done: come to Jesus. Put him into your heart, and then think of this wonderful Savior.

There's a star in the sky, and that wonderful star is pointing to Jesus. I hope and I pray that you put your faith in the Lord Jesus, and if you do, then just draw closer to him and keep your eye on that star. Let that be your guide in life, that wonderful Savior. He loves you. and he'll help you.

Jesus: Our Born King

Dear heavenly Father, we rejoice when we read of the birth of your dear Son, and what a gift that was for you to give to our world. What a wonderful Savior he was, that he was willing to come and to be born of the virgin. He was born the same way we are, except he didn't have sin, and he came because he loved us, and so we have Christmas when Jesus came.

We want to pray today that you'll help us be sure that we know the Savior. And then, like the wise men, that we search him out, and that we love him and worship him.

We want to pray for those who have special needs. I know there are those who have lost loved ones, and there are those who have maybe lost their job, and they're looking for work. There are others who may have problems in the home or at work, and things aren't well. Maybe it's financial needs. Dear God, you know everything about every one of us. The hairs of our head are numbered, that's how much you know about us. So bless each one, and help us to lean on you. Help us to thank you that you promised that you would never leave us or forsake us, and no matter where we go or what we face, you are with us, and when we come to the end of life and we leave this world, you are with us.

We're never alone, and you take us right on into heaven where we'll see a great host of loved ones who've been worshiping you all around the world.

In Jesus' name, we pray, amen.

Peter:
Peace During
the Storm

12

Peter:
Peace During the Storm
Matthew 14:22-33

²² And straightway Jesus constrained his disciples to get into a ship, and to go before him unto the other side, while he sent the multitudes away.

²³ And when he had sent the multitudes away, he went up into a mountain apart to pray: and when the evening was come, he was there alone.

²⁴ But the ship was now in the midst of the sea, tossed with waves: for the wind was contrary.

²⁵ And in the fourth watch of the night Jesus went unto them, walking on the sea.

²⁶ And when the disciples saw him walking on the sea, they were troubled, saying, It is a spirit; and they cried out for fear.

²⁷ But straightway Jesus spake unto them, saying, Be of good cheer; it is I; be not afraid.

²⁸ And Peter answered him and said, Lord, if it be thou, bid me come unto thee on the water.

²⁹ And he said, Come. And when Peter was come down out of the ship, he walked on the water, to go to Jesus.

³⁰ But when he saw the wind boisterous, he was afraid; and beginning to sink, he cried, saying, Lord, save me.

³¹ And immediately Jesus stretched forth his hand, and caught him, and said unto him, O thou of little faith, wherefore didst thou doubt?

³² And when they were come into the ship, the wind ceased.

³³ Then they that were in the ship came and worshipped him, saying, Of a truth thou art the Son of God.

I LOVE TO PREACH ABOUT PETER WALKING ON THE WATER. It's a story about the disciples. Here they were in the midst of a storm. They were afraid. They were afraid they were going to perish, and they were at their wit's end.

Have you ever felt like that? Have you ever had a time when you just didn't know what to do, which way to turn? Well, let me tell you, if you haven't been in that situation, just wait a little bit, and you will be. Because there are storms in life, and life never stays the same. So we've got to face the storms. And the question is, What are you going to do when you face them? When you're in them? Because you're going to be in them.

The disciples were sent on this voyage, you'll remember, after Jesus preached to the multitude. He sent them on the voyage while he dismissed the multitude, who went to their homes. Then we read, "He went up into a mountain apart to pray. And when the evening was come, he was there alone" (Matthew 14:23). So Jesus had a time for prayer. He sent the disciples, putting them in the boat and telling them to go across to the other side, and then he left them and went up into the mountain to pray.

And I want to simply say that if Jesus had to pray, why wouldn't we have to pray? The secret of it all is getting alone with God and talking with God. I'm telling you, there's more power in prayer than we ever realized.

So Jesus was praying.

So the disciples got into the boat, and we're told that he commanded and insisted that they go. So they did as he told them. Then we're told in verse 24, "But the ship was now in the midst of the sea tossed with waves, for the wind was contrary." The disciples were fighting some hard going. The wind was fierce and the waves were tumultuous.

I think this story gives us the answer to the storms of life. How did Jesus handle them? How did the disciples handle them? How are we going to handle them?

The story recorded by Matthew begins with these words: "Straightway Jesus constrained his disciples to get into a ship and go to the other side." He constrained them. He made them go; they had to go.

Then in verse 25: "In the fourth watch of the night, Jesus went unto them walking on the sea." There was a fierce storm raging. The disciples were in this boat, and they saw the winds and the waves, and they were afraid of going under. Now these were fishermen, and when you can scare a fisherman, it must be a bad storm.

In the midst of it all, they saw Jesus walking on the sea. The fourth watch of the night meant that these men had been rowing and toiling about nine hours, but they'd gone only about three and a half miles. The men of the sea were having trouble with the sea, and they didn't know which way to turn, which way to go.

We read, "And so, when the disciples saw him walking on the sea, they were troubled, saying, It is a spirit; and they cried out for fear." It was about three or four o'clock in the morning, and it was dark. Then all of a sudden, in that darkness, somehow there was light shining on them. Jesus was shining—or something. Because they saw him.

The waves were wild, and it's a terrible storm, and there he was, walking on that water. They thought it was a spirit. They thought it was a ghost. They couldn't imagine it was Jesus, because he was up on the mountaintop praying for them. They were already scared half to death by the storm, but now they were scared even more by this ghost or whatever it was.

"And straightway Jesus says unto them, Be of good cheer" (verse 27). "Be of good cheer, it is I. Be not afraid." Jesus didn't leave them in their anxious fears. He said, "Be not afraid." Jesus was always saying that to his people. Don't be afraid. Don't be afraid.

People fear many things: "I don't know about old age." "I don't know how I'm going to pay my bills." "I don't know about my health." *Don't fear*—Jesus is always telling you that. He doesn't want us to be fearful. Perfect love casts out fear. So we just trust Jesus and lean on him.

Peter answered him and said, "Lord, if it be thou, bid me come unto thee on the water." Some people say that Peter is presumptuous here to make such a request, but I don't think so. Jesus knew the heart. So we're told that Jesus said, "Come." And when Peter stepped out of the boat, he walked on the water to go to Jesus. But when he saw the boisterous wind, he was afraid, and he began to sink. He cried out, saying, "Lord, save me."

Peter stepped out on the water in faith. I think he walked a long way on that water. I don't think he took just two steps and went under. I think he actually walked on water just like Jesus. He was going to Jesus, and then he looked around, and he saw that he was going to sink. He said, "Lord, Jesus, save me." And immediately Jesus stretched forth his hand and caught him and said unto him, "O thou of little faith, wherefore didst thou doubt?" Jesus saved him immediately. But Jesus also rebuked him for not having faith: "Peter, you shouldn't doubt; that's why you're sinking. You're doubting." God help me not to doubt.

When they were come into the ship, the winds ceased. There was another miracle. It teaches us that Jesus is the master of the sea; he walks on it. And Jesus is master of the wind; it stops. He's God Almighty. All of nature obeys him and does as he wills and as he says. Then we read that those who were in the ship came and worshiped him. They said, "Of a truth, thou art the Son of God." Worship was his due, and they worshiped him and praised his name.

From this beautiful and informative story, I want you to see three things.

First, I want you to see that there are going to be storms in this life. You're not going to get through it without those storms.

I see the little children in Sunday school, and I love those little children. I see them and I often think, "Oh, my dear Jesus, I wish they would never have a trouble in their life. I wish they'd never have to cry. I wish there wouldn't be a storm." But there's going to be storms. They're going to have to face them.

Those storms are going to be with us. Jesus told us there would be storms. He lived through them. Jesus lived through his storms. He went through Gethsemane. What a storm that was!

And what a horrible storm, when he took upon himself the sins of the world. He was on Calvary, and there he was nailed to the cross, naked before the world. He warned his disciples, and he said, "Listen, I've got my trials and my troubles." And he says in John 16:33, "In the world you're going to have tribulation. But be of good courage, I have overcome the world."

And remember the words of Peter, who talks about those battles. He wrote, "Beloved, think it not strange concerning the fiery trial which is to try you, as though some strange thing happened unto you; but rejoice, inasmuch as ye are partakers of Christ's sufferings, that when his glory shall be revealed, ye may be glad also with exceeding joy" (1 Peter 4:12-13).

Let me point you out something. When we go through some storm, we sometimes think it's because we're being punished for some sin, or that we're out of God's will—one of the two. Well, those disciples were in the center of God's will. They were right where they should be. Jesus had said, "Get in that boat and cross." That was his will, and they obeyed, and now they were in the storm.

So when you face that storm of life, don't think God is punishing you for past sins, because those sins were washed away. Now if those sins brought on lung cancer or something, then you have to pay that. But God isn't going to punish you twice for your sins, when he forgives you; those past sins are forgiven.

Don't think that when you're in the will of God, you're always going to have a perfect job, and a parking place right by the door of the grocery store, and perfect health, and all the rest. That health and wealth is not in the Bible. It isn't in the Bible, because the disciples were God's people, and they were in God's will, and they were in a horrible time. They were about to die.

In Hebrews 11, we read about some of God's heroes of the faith: "They were stoned. They were sawn asunder. They were tempted. They were slain with the sword. They wandered about in sheepskins and goatskins. They were destitute, afflicted, and tormented." That's people in the midst of many storms—but they're walking in the will of God, and living for God and for Jesus Christ, and they're carrying out his will. So the storms are going to come. We don't know exactly when or for how long, but the storms are coming.

The storms of life are thrust upon us, and sometimes they're of our own making. But often it's not our making at all. It's the will of a loving God, to help us live for him, to serve him for some purpose in that way.

But we're victims of the storm, so we try to evade it. We try to diffuse it. We try to manage it, or get around it. But the storms of life are going to be there.

The second thing we want to look at is that Jesus is with us in the storm. The disciples had been sent to cross the Sea of Galilee. Jesus stayed behind to pray. Consequently, they felt that he was still on the shore behind them while they were in the storm. They were feeling they were all alone. They were feeling that Jesus didn't know what they were up against, that he didn't understand that they were in trouble. He was somewhere praying on the mountaintop. But lo and behold, all the time Jesus had his eye on his struggling children, and he was with them. He knew all about their problems. He knew all about their storms. He was with them.

Have you ever felt like God didn't hear your prayers? And worse yet, that he didn't care about your troubles and trials? Well, if you felt that way, you felt wrong. Because Jesus is never far away from us. He's always with us, walking beside us, and helping us. He will never leave us or forsake us. Praise Jesus. Wonderful, wonderful Jesus.

You may not see him, you may not feel him, you may not hear him. But bless you, he is there by your side. Remember Shadrach, Meshach, and Abednego? They were cast into the fiery furnace. That was their storm. In the midst of the storm, they thought they were all by themselves, but there was a fourth person. Jesus, in his preincarnate form, was with them in the furnace of life.

He will always be with us that way. He has not forgotten you. You may be alone, or sick, or weary, or your children aren't behaving, or you got a divorce, or you can't pay your bills. And you pray, but you may think, "I don't think Jesus hears me." But Jesus is never very far away. He's always there. He knows what you're going through. He never slumbers or sleeps. His eye is ever upon you. His arm is always around you. His heart beats with yours. He's a wonderful, wonderful Savior.

And he never abandons us. He never forsakes us. We forsake him. I've failed the Lord a hundred times over. I've failed the Lord and forsaken the Lord, but he sees me through the darkest night and the fiercest storm. He's always with me. He keeps his promise given so long ago by the prophet Isaiah:

> Do not be afraid, for I have ransomed you. I have called you by my name; you are mine. When you go through the deep waters, I will be with thee. When you go through rivers of difficulty, you will not drown. When you walk through the fire of oppression, you will not be burned up; the flames will not consume you. (Isaiah 43:1-2 NLT)

Remember, Jesus Christ is with us, close to us. And you need to personally know him. Just ask him into your heart, and he will never leave you or forsake you. He's always there.

I read the cute little story told by Judy Zamoreland of Edina, Minnesota, about Katie, her three-year-old daughter. Little Katie was taken to the pediatrician during a recent bout with flu. As the doctor examined her ears, he said, "Will I find Big Bird in here?" Apprehensively Katie said, "Well, no." Then while examining her throat, he said, "Will I find the Cookie Monster here?" And Katie again said, "Well, no." Finally, listening to her heart he said, "Will I hear Barney in here?" With innocent conviction she looked the doctor right in his eye and said, "No, Jesus is in my heart. Barney's on my underwear."

Dear friend, be like Katie. Jesus is with you, and he'll never leave you or forsake you. In the storms of life Jesus—blessed, beautiful Jesus—is there.

Then finally, Jesus is our only help in the time of storm.

Those storms are too big for us. They're too fierce. We can't stand up and beat them alone. There's no way, they're too complex, and sometimes the things in life are too complicated. Satan is very wise, and he stirs up storms about us that overwhelm us. Don't try to get out of the fire. Don't try to get out of the storm. You cannot do it. You cannot beat it. But look at this: Jesus can keep you.

Just like he saved Peter from the waters, Jesus is there for you if you will just believe. Just trust Jesus. No matter how close the dear Lord Jesus is, the faith must be in the disciple. We have to trust him. He can't help us if we don't trust him. He couldn't help Peter when Peter didn't trust him. So put your faith in Jesus, and Jesus can work with you.

Peter was actually walking on the water until he looked about him, and then he took his eyes off Jesus. So we read, "When Peter was come down out of the ship, he walked on the water, to go to Jesus" (Matthew 14:29). Jesus was off there in the distance, and Peter was walking to Jesus. As a matter of fact, he walked all the way to Jesus, and Jesus just had to take his hand to reach him. He was there.

"But when he saw the wind boisterous he was afraid, and beginning to sink he cried saying, Lord, save me" (14:30). You see, Peter began to look around and beneath. He took his eyes off Jesus in order to look at all the things about him. The minute he took his eyes off Jesus, he was in trouble.

But if you keep your eyes on Jesus, you can walk on water. You seek to please him in your life, and you trust him, and you give your heart and soul to him, and you never worry, you never fret. You can stop thinking about the difficulties and the duties and the troubles of life—and the storm—and just keep your eyes on Jesus.

In the old days of the sailing vessels, when a new man, a new hand, climbed the narrow rope ladder to the crow's nest, it was high and it was weaving, and climbing it was tiresome. It was a hard thing to do. The old hands would always cry to the rookie going up for the first time and say, "Look up. Look up." If the lad looked down he might become dizzy and fall. But if he looked up, he could get to the goal; he could win the day.

All through life, dear friend, look up. Look up to Jesus. You can weather the storm, you can go through anything. He will never give us more than we can bear, but we have to look up and keep our eyes on Jesus.

The next time you wonder why God has allowed these things to come into your life, and you feel that God has forsaken you and is a million miles away, just remember this: he's always there. You may not see him, feel him, understand him. You may not know why. He promised that he would never leave you or forsake you. Take heart. Move on. Live for Jesus.

But you can't do it if you don't have Jesus. You can't trust in him if you don't know him. You have to know him personally. And you know him personally by saying, "Dear Jesus, I'm a poor lost sinner. I'm in a storm and I'm lost. I ask you to come into my heart; take away my sins, dear Jesus. I'll follow you, I'll forsake anything evil in my life. I'll live just for you the best I can. And thank you, Jesus."

If you pray that, you're a child of God. You've been baptized by the Holy Spirit, and you're in the body of Christ. Your name is written in the

Lamb's Book of Life, and you'll live forever. He'll never leave you or forsake you. Maybe you're going through troubles today; just get your eyes on Jesus. Don't look around, don't pay any attention to the bills and all the rest of it, and all that's happening, the evil things. Just get your eyes on Jesus.

Dear heavenly Father, we thank you for the multitudes of people who have prayed that prayer. We believe that all over the world people are praying that prayer and being born again, and they're children of God right now. So we pray for them. We pray as they start in their Christian life. We pray for those on beds of sickness, we pray for those in wheelchairs. We pray for those who are lonely, and they're aged, and they can't get around, and can't do things anymore. Help them to know that you are there, and to get their eyes on Jesus, and know that he will help and strengthen them. And dear Lord, we pray that in all things we'll do your will, your holy will, in Jesus' name.

Thank you for this wonderful story of how Peter walked on the water. O Lord, help us to learn never to take our eyes off of you, but to rest in you and lean upon you. And we can do all things as we rely upon your leadership and guidance. Help us honor you, our beautiful, wonderful Jesus.

In his name, amen.

The Prodigal Son:
God's Great Love

12

The Prodigal Son:
God's Great Love

Luke 15:11-24

IN LUKE 15:11-24 WE FIND THE PARABLE OF THE PRODIGAL SON.

¹¹ And he said, A certain man had two sons:

¹² And the younger of them said to his father, Father, give me the portion of goods that falleth to me. And he divided unto them his living.

¹³ And not many days after the younger son gathered all together, and took his journey into a far country, and there wasted his substance with riotous living.

¹⁴ And when he had spent all, there arose a mighty famine in that land; and he began to be in want.

¹⁵ And he went and joined himself to a citizen of that country; and he sent him into his fields to feed swine.

¹⁶ And he would fain have filled his belly with the husks that the swine did eat: and no man gave unto him.

¹⁷ And when he came to himself, he said, How many hired servants of my father's have bread enough and to spare, and I perish with hunger!

¹⁸ I will arise and go to my father, and will say unto him, Father, I have sinned against heaven, and before thee,

¹⁹ And am no more worthy to be called thy son: make me as one of thy hired servants.

²⁰ And he arose, and came to his father. But when he was yet a great way off, his father saw him, and had compassion, and ran, and fell on his neck, and kissed him.

²¹ And the son said unto him, Father, I have sinned against heaven, and in thy sight, and am no more worthy to be called thy son.

²² But the father said to his servants, Bring forth the best robe, and put it on him; and put a ring on his hand, and shoes on his feet:

²³ And bring hither the fatted calf, and kill it; and let us eat, and be merry:

²⁴ For this my son was dead, and is alive again; he was lost, and is found. And they began to be merry.

Jesus sometimes gave parables to sinners and sometimes he gave them to just the Christians. The parable of the prodigal son is given to unbelievers, as we see in Luke 15:1-2, which says, "Then drew unto him all the publicans and sinners for to hear him. And the Pharisees and scribes murmured, saying, This man receiveth sinners, and eateth with them." So this parable is given to publicans and sinners, Pharisees and scribes. It's a story of how fellowship between a father and son was broken because of the son's sinful pride, and how that fellowship was later restored.

I love to preach this parable, and I don't know how many times I've preached it. It's the gospel, and the gospel says that there's nobody helpless. There's not a case of anybody who has gone so far that they can't be saved. Unless you're dead, of course, because after death, it's the judgment. Then it's all settled.

But if you want to be saved, if you want to be washed clean of your sins, and you want to come to Jesus, you can pray. Ask Jesus to come into your life and tell him you're a sinner. Tell him what your sins are, then ask him to forgive you. Then get your Bible, and start walking with the Lord and serving him.

The first thing I want to point out in this parable is that the son's squandering of the fortune he was given is not what made him a prodigal. His living with the harlots didn't make him a prodigal. His tending of the pigs, even though he was a Jewish boy, didn't make him a prodigal.

He became a prodigal the moment his disobeyed his father and left his home. That made him the prodigal.

Dr. Harry Ironside points that out. He says, "It's not a question of the amount of sin that one commits that makes him a prodigal. This young man was just as truly a sinner against his father's love the moment he crossed the threshold of the door as he was in the far country."[7]

Sometimes people think, "Well, there are certain degrees of sin, and this young man had the worst kind." Just remember this: God says that in his sight, sin is sin. In our sight, we think of little sins and big sins. We've got them all categorized. "This is a terrible sin. But if you tell a little white lie then that's not so bad." But as far as God is concerned, "He that offended the law in one point is guilty of all." So if you break one of the commandments, you're guilty of breaking all of them.

This young man in the parable committed a sin. The type of sin doesn't make a particle of difference. For instance, you take Adam and Eve in the garden of Eden. Their sin was not wild parties and drinking. And it wasn't a sin of adultery. What was their sin? Well, we read in the Bible that it was disobedience, pure and simple. God said, "Don't eat of that tree." Adam said, "I ate of that tree." There's your sin—disobedience.

We have to be very careful, because maybe we've been disobedient, and maybe God is saying something to our heart, and maybe he's told us that a certain thing is wrong. He reminds us it's wrong to carry a grudge, but we carry a grudge and won't forgive someone. Disobedience is just as great a sin as any sin you'd want to mention.

In the parable, the younger son displays rebellion against his father, and he doesn't want to wait for his inheritance.

Now, he had an inheritance coming. Nowadays, you don't know what these older folks are going do with their inheritance. They might spend it on a big trip or something, and their kids don't get anything. But in those days, they didn't do that; they passed it on to their children.

This young man is going to get an inheritance. He has an older brother who's also going to get an inheritance. But the young fellow thought to himself, "I would just like to live without the influence of my father. I don't like his rules and I don't like his regulations." Just like people don't like God's rules and regulations. They want to break them and get away from God. The young man says, "I just want to be my own boss. I want to have liberty. I want to live without any restrictions."

Have you heard that before? I don't know about other countries, but in America I know that this attitude is prevalent everywhere: "Don't you tell me what I can do or can't do. I'm an American, and I can live as I like." They rule God out of their life.

The younger son wants to flee the influence of his father, and he wants his inheritance. Then he can be free and independent. The inheritance is eventually going be his anyway, but he says, "I don't want to wait. I just want to get going now, and I want to live it up while I'm young. If I get old, I can't do some of the things I want to do. I just want my money now."

So he goes to the father. The young man shows rebellion against his father. We see this in our own life—rebellion against God. How many times do we read of people shaking their fist in the face of God and telling him, "You can't rule my life and tell me what I need to do"? That's so prevalent.

The young man wants to get outside the influence of his father, so he goes into a foreign country. Now he's his own boss. He can do his own thing. He's footloose and fancy-free. That's the way the sinner is today. They want to get out from under the influence of God. They don't want to read the Bible. They don't want the Ten Commandments anywhere. They don't want them in the schools. Now, I think it would make a big difference in school behavior if they'd display those Ten Commandments and read them every day and learn to memorize them. But no, they can't go into the schools today unless it's a Christian school.

So this young man takes his inheritance. He moves out, and he disappears, and he goes to this far-off country. And he's living there as high and mighty as he can, and just having a great time. He's attracting a lot of friends, and he's got a lot of pretty ladies coming around, because they know he has money, and so he's really celebrating. He's buying and he's gambling, and he's doing everything—just a riotous living. He has that precious inheritance, but that money is dwindling away pretty fast, and pretty soon it's dissipated. It's all gone.

Does he go live with his friends? Oh, no. When he doesn't have any money, those type of friends are long gone. He doesn't see them anymore.

He has no food and he's starving. He's too proud to beg. He's not going to be begging, because he comes from a high-class family. He's used to having a lot of money, so he's not going to beg.

He gets a job, and it's a job herding pigs. This is a terrible thing for this poor young man. He's a Jewish boy. Swine are unclean animals, and the boy's family would never have had them on the place, let alone have him taking care of them. But in his lowered position, he got this job feeding the pigs, and he's living with them.

Meanwhile the father has suffered a great loss by his son's departure. He doesn't know where his boy is, but he knows his boy is gone. He knows his boy is living a hard life. Surely he wonders how he's going to get along. Maybe somebody's going to rob and kill him to get his money. Or maybe he's going to run out of money, and then what would he live on?

I'm going to tell you something. That father at home suffered just as much as the boy. You know, if something difficult happens to your son or your daughter, you tell yourself, "I wish that thing could be on me instead of my precious child. I wish that I could be sick, I wish that I could have that infirmity, instead of my child." When your children suffer, you suffer just as much more than they do.

When I was raised, they used to spank. My mother would promise to spank if we didn't listen to her. My dad would get mad at us, and he'd threaten us, but if we could stay out of his way for just ten minutes, then he never touched us. But my little German mother—if she said she would spank us, then we got a spanking.

Well, you could try outrunning her; she couldn't catch you. But when it got dark outside, and the owl would hoot, you'd head home. And there was the stick. You got your spanking. And she would say, "This hurts me more than it does you." We could never believe that.

But when you see your children hurt, when you see your children suffer, you suffer as much as they do, or more than they do.

That's what this poor father is doing. He's thinking about his son, and the son is off living a hard life. This father is thinking about his son, but his son isn't thinking about him. He wants to live his own life. He doesn't want the father to have anything to do with him; he just lives as he wants to.

As I grew up as a boy, I was kept out of a lot of sin because I didn't want to disappoint my mother. Not all sin, don't get me wrong. But I was kept out of a lot of sin because of that. My mother was a real influence in my life. I've committed my share of sins, but I tell you, they would have been a lot worse and more numerous if it hadn't been for her love for me, and her belief in me, and her prayers for me. I remember when my mother died, I wondered, Who is going to pray for me now? While she was alive, there was always somebody praying for me, and that was a source of a lot of strength.

Well, I found out that in my wonderful church, there were a lot of people praying for me. And the old mothers and the grandmothers— how they would pray! The old grandpas were about fishing or hunting or running around, as a rule—there were some exceptions. It was usually the grandmothers and the mothers who prayed, and those prayers made a lot of difference.

I'm sure this father prayed, and he wished that his boy could just come home.

Here is this boy; look at him for a minute. He's proud, he's headstrong, he's high-minded. He thought he could find liberty and freedom when he got off into a foreign country, and that he could live like he wanted, but he strikes out. Now he's out of money.

Then Jesus said, "And when he had spent all, there arose a great famine in that country." So now the boy wasn't eating. He had to get a job taking care of the pigs. That was humiliating and degrading for him, and then he'd have to eat with the pigs. The pigs left some husks, so his supper would be corn husks with swine drool, something like that. How would you like to eat after a hog? We used to have hogs in our place, and I'd tell you, I'd have to be awful hungry to eat after them. But that's what he was doing.

Then, here's the bright spot in the story. Jesus said, "He came to himself." It's a glorious thing when a man comes to himself. That means he comes to his senses, he's thinking right, he's figuring right. And when a man comes to his senses, he'll turn to the Lord. He'll straighten out. He'll come back to God.

Many a time I've seen people live their life and then, all of a sudden, after they've had everything going so fine, the bottom drops out. Maybe the loss of a loved one. Maybe the loss of a child. But they have everything gone, and then they come to themselves, and they can see all. "I've been working for nothing. I've been working for something that vanishes like the morning mist. I don't have a thing." And they come to Christ, and put themselves into his care.

One of the best men I ever knew was someone named Carp. He didn't live for the Lord at all. He got sick and he got down and out, and he turned to Christ, and he eventually became a deacon in the church. I'm going to be glad to see Carp again, a dear man.

In the parable, this boy came to himself, so he went back to his father and to his home. When he arrives back home, the father runs to him and falls on his neck and kisses him. I want to tell you something, friend: in the Middle East, this just isn't done. In the Middle East, there's respect for old age, and the old man would never run to the boy; the boy comes to his father; the younger comes to the elder. That's just the order of things in the Middle East, and I've experienced that and seen that.

But in this parable, the old father sees him a long ways down the road. Jesus said, "When he was a great way off, his father saw him." And I wonder if that old dad had been sitting out in front of that house every day, looking down that road—every day, till that boy came home.

I talked to a man whose son was killed in an accident about thirty years ago. I asked him, "Do you ever think of your son?" And he said, "Every day."

This father is here and he's sitting day after day, and he's waiting. He sees a speck down the road. He gets his spyglasses and he looks, and sure enough, it's his son. That's all that it took. He drops his glasses, and the old man runs down that dirt road, and he comes to his son and falls on his neck and kisses him. He smothered him with kisses.

Now, that's a picture of the heavenly Father—this old man running to a besmirched lad. That's how much Jesus Christ cares for you! He's not willing that any should perish, but that all should come to repentance. Jesus died for all of us, and when one of those people comes to salvation, Jesus and the Father rejoice.

It says in the Scriptures that there is rejoicing of the angels in heaven in the presence of God. The angels are rejoicing, but also God the Father, God the Son, and God the Holy Spirit are rejoicing for every saved soul! Because each soul is worth more than everything in the whole universe put together. It is worth the blood of Jesus Christ.

The father runs to the son, and he takes him and he kisses him. We'd probably say to that father, "Well, your son smells like a pig. He's been with pigs. Why don't you have him cleaned up first? I wouldn't touch him. He's probably got diseases. He's probably got AIDS, or maybe he's got swine flu or something. Don't get near him."

But the old father is saying, "Let me hold him. Let me embrace him. Let me love him. He can clean up afterwards."

Dr. Ironside put it this way:

> He cried out in his joy, "Bring forth the best robe and put it on him." For us that robe is Christ perfection.
>
> "Put a ring on his hand." The ring tells of undying affection.
>
> "Put shoes on his feet." Slaves went barefooted. Sons wore shoes.
>
> "Bring here the fatted calf and kill it. Let us eat and be merry for this my son was dead and is alive again. He was lost and he is found." They began to make merry and that merriment never ended. [8]

The celebration may have ended, but that merriment in the heart of that father and that son went on as long as they lived, and it went on in heaven. The father is rejoicing over that son who went astray.

That's why we ought to be witnessing, and trying to talk to other people, and helping them come to know Jesus Christ. Because they mean so much to God. If we knew God's heart, I tell you, we would witness to more people and bring more people to church and get those little children into Sunday school, so they can come to know the Lord.

That father says, "My son was lost and is found." They had communion together. They had merriment together, and it lasted forever and ever.

I want to tell you something. That's the way God is today. I've been in the work of ministry for a while. I've had people tell me over and over, "Well, I want to quit smoking before I join the church, before I accept the Lord. I don't want to be a hypocrite. I want to get rid of this habit. I have a little habit of drinking. I want to get something else straightened out in my life. I want to pay my debts first."

But God is saying, "You just come—as filthy, and dirty, and lousy, and stinking as you are."

You come, and he'll put his arms around you. He'll embrace you, and he'll help you. He wants you to clean up your heart and clean up your attitude and clean up your life. That will come. But believe me, dear friends, he will receive you now. So don't you worry about whether you're too bad for God.

Like the poor woman I knew who thought that if she was baptized, the water would turn black. She'd had a terrible life. But she put her faith in Christ, and Jesus put his arms around her the minute she made that prayer.

He'll do the same for you. So why would you wait? Why would you put it off?

You need to pray, and just say, "Dear Jesus, I'm a poor lost sinner." He knows it, but he wants you to confess it. Just tell him you're a sinner. Like this boy, tell him that you're a sinner. You've done evil things. Tell him what they are if you want. Then ask him to cleanse you with his blood and to wash away your sin, and he'll save you. He'll save you from all your sins. He'll help you to clean up. All your life, you'll be working on it—cleaning up your life.

I remember one time when I was thinking that I wished I could be a good Christian, a perfect Christian. I accepted the Lord when I was ten years old, and I used to get mad at the cows. We used to milk cows. I don't know where my dad got those cows; they were wild and crazy things. But you could get them for about ten dollars a head. And we would milk those cows. I used to get so mad at them, and I thought, "Oh, if I could just get my temper under control, I'd be a perfect Christian."

I worked on my temper. And I thought I had it under control, but then there was something else that wasn't right. I was envious. I was jealous. I was a dozen different things.

All your life, you're going to have a struggle. And I'm going tell you a little secret. The closer you get to Jesus, the more flaws you're going to see. So you just work on it. You're never going to be perfect in this life. But we strive toward that. We work toward that, and God helps us.

In the parable, they have this wonderful party. But the prodigal son has an elder brother, and his elder brother represents the Pharisees. Now remember, Jesus has the Pharisees listening to this story, and he's got the scribes, and he's got the sinners, and he's got the publicans. The sinners and the publicans, they're represented in that young man who sinned and then repented and returned home. They come to Jesus.

You remember the two men who went to the temple and prayed—the publican and the Pharisee. And the Pharisee went way up front, and he made a fancy prayer. But the publican stood in the back and he beat upon his breast and said, "God, be merciful to me, a sinner." And Jesus said that this publican went down to his house justified, but not the Pharisee.

With this parable of the prodigal son, Jesus is talking directly to these proud Pharisees. They think they are so spiritual, that they knew the law so perfectly. So he talks to them, and he's telling them this older brother: "Look, he's angry." In the story, the older brother was so angry with how his father was treating his younger brother that he wouldn't go in to the celebration. Therefore his father came out and entreated him.

But he wouldn't come in. He was mad because, he had stayed home. He didn't spend his money on the harlots. He didn't throw away his fortune. He stuck right there and he worked for his dad. He kept the law. He did the things of God. He was busy doing the right things. But you know, he's self-righteous.

He didn't have the father's heart. If he had the father's heart, he'd love his younger brother. Instead of being angry that he came home, he would have been rejoicing. So we have those people who think they're so spiritual, but they don't have any burden for the backslider. They don't have any heart for the lost. They don't understand the heart of God. They don't get near to the heart of God.

We see this elder brother, and he's so passionate about making clear that he's nothing like his brother. And his father is saying, "Oh my son. I've always had you with me. I love you. But this is your brother, I have to take him in. I have to have him come in and be with me." And the older brother would have nothing to do with it.

See, the older brother is like the legalist. He's self-righteous. He's never understood the grace of God. He's never caught on. When he talks about this brother to his father, he calls him "your son"; he doesn't call him "my brother." He separates himself from his brother, because he didn't have the father's heart.

The Pharisees were morally good people, but they were arrogant and self-righteous. They thought they were better than anybody else. They would never look at the poor sinner, the poor publican. They wouldn't even eat with such a one.

Jesus is teaching them, as they're sitting there, that you have to have the heart of God. This older brother looks upon himself as a perfect son because he has done all the right things. He didn't go and do all the wrong things his brother did. "But your son—just look at what he's done!"

The elder brother never caught on. He never had a heart of love. He never cared. He didn't have grace. He didn't have mercy. And he wouldn't come in to celebrate his brother's return, though his father talked to him and tried to persuade him.

With this parable, Jesus is talking to the Pharisees, and he's talking to us, telling us that we need to be very careful. As we live for the Lord and love the Lord, we need to be careful that we're trusting him, and leaning on him, and getting his heart, and getting a burden for the lost.

These poor people, we see them every day. I see some of these people in town when I go around, and I wonder sometimes, Do they know the Lord? I don't talk to them. I preach to them. But it's easier to preach to people than it is to talk face to face and person to person. But we have that burden, where we have an opportunity; we don't judge these people, but we just pray for them and see if they can't come in and come back to know the Lord.

Are you searching in a far-off country today for these things? Searching for the things of the world? Do you think you can have a good time because you cut the Lord out of your life? How do you live? Where do you go Saturday nights? What do you read? What kind of movies do you watch? What kind of music do you listen to? Are you running with the world's crowd, with liquor and all the rest of it—all the evil things?

If you're a young person, you especially have to be very careful. Because if you run with the wrong crowd, they're going to affect you, and you're going to move that way. You're going to lean that way.

I remember one time, I saw some carnations and they were blue. I'd never seen anything but a white carnation, and then I saw a green carnation. I couldn't understand how in the world there could be a green carnation.

Then I found out what they do. They take the carnation and they set it in dye—green or blue. Then a few days later, that beautiful flower that was so white and pure and clean is discolored in some other color.

When we run with those people, that's what happens. And that's why we have to be careful when we watch television, because television has affected the whole human. Wherever it's at, it has affected them. Most of the time it has taken people down. We have to be so careful that we don't get caught up in it. Live your life with godly people, and walk with godly people.

Like this prodigal son, come to your senses, and come back to God. When we come back to God, he'll receive us and accept us. There will be joy and there will be happiness.

I read about John Bunyan. He was a profane man. By profession he was a tinker—that is, he would go to people's houses and he'd sharpen your knives and your scissors, and fix up little things that needed fixing. But when he came up the streets, the mothers would pull their children indoors, because the man was so profane. But that man came to know Jesus, and he was born again and served the Lord. I'm praying that you come today.

Dear Lord, I want to thank you for this parable. It tells us that no matter what we have done, no matter how sinful we've been, you will gladly receive us if we come to you, repenting of our sins and confessing our sins to you. We think of Saul of Tarsus and how he persecuted the church. He put Christians to death, and yet you saved him by your grace. And so I'm just so thankful that we can have a message that says, "Though your sins be as scarlet, they can be as white as snow." It doesn't matter what they are.

Lord, I want to also pray for those who may be having troubles today. Help them know that you love them and care for them.

In this wonderful parable of the prodigal son, we see your wonderful grace and mercy. So bless us.

In Jesus' name, amen.

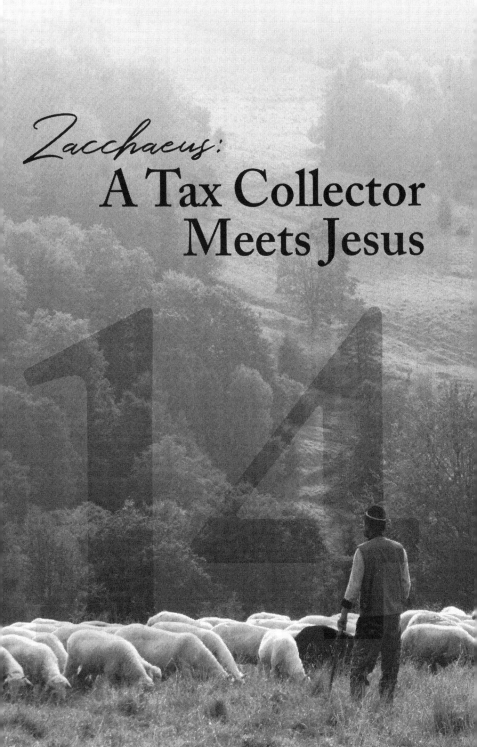

Zacchaeus:
A Tax Collector
Meets Jesus

14

Zacchaeus:
A Tax Collector Meets Jesus

Luke 19:1-10

[1] And Jesus entered and passed through Jericho.

[2] And, behold, there was a man named Zacchaeus, which was the chief among the publicans, and he was rich.

[3] And he sought to see Jesus who he was; and could not for the press, because he was little of stature.

[4] And he ran before, and climbed up into a sycamore tree to see him: for he was to pass that way.

[5] And when Jesus came to the place, he looked up, and saw him, and said unto him, Zacchaeus, make haste, and come down; for today I must abide at thy house.

[6] And he made haste, and came down, and received him joyfully.

[7] And when they saw it, they all murmured, saying, that he was gone to be guest with a man that is a sinner.

[8] And Zacchaeus stood, and said unto the Lord: Behold, Lord, the half of my goods I give to the poor; and if I have taken any thing from any man by false accusation, I restore him fourfold.

[9] And Jesus said unto him, This day is salvation come to this house, forsomuch as he also is a son of Abraham.

[10] For the Son of man is come to seek and to save that which was lost.

THIS IS A STORY I'VE PREACHED I DON'T KNOW HOW MANY TIMES, but it changes every time for me. As you get older, you have a little different perspective.

It's a story about a dirty little politician. He was caught up in a tree just like a polecat, and he was a despicable person. But his story has a wonderful, wonderful ending. I always like stories with good endings.

That's why I like preaching the gospel. It always has a good ending. I never have to end and say, "Well, you've committed an unpardonable sin," or, "You've gone too far," or, "You just can't make it; there's just too much sin in your life; your heart is too black." No, I can end on a high note every time I preach the gospel, because God is not willing that any should perish, but that all should come to repentance, and that includes the worst of sinners.

Let's look at this story of Zacchaeus. Jesus was traveling, and he was going through Samaria to Jerusalem. It was toward the end of his ministry, of his life on earth. In just a few days, he would be hanging on that old rugged cross. So he was on the way to Jerusalem. And he went through Jericho.

Now, Jericho is not on a straight route from Samaria to Jerusalem. Jesus goes out of his way to go through Jericho, because there's a man in Jericho that Jesus wants to talk to. He wants to save him, and so he goes out of his way to meet him. He is a little short man, and a very rich man. He's a man people hated with a passion. They hated him because he was the chief publican, which is a tax collector. He worked for the Roman government. The Romans hired these local tax collectors, and this man happened to be a Jew, and he's collecting money from Jews to give to the hated Romans, who were Gentiles. The Jews hated him for doing that, but also because he took extra money. The Roman government would say, "All right, Zacchaeus, this is your area." They would tell him how much money they wanted to receive from this area, and then they would say, "Whatever you collect over that amount, you get to keep." So Zacchaeus would use the power of the Roman government to cheat his own people and enrich himself.

William Barclay writes,

> A tax-collector could bid a man to stop on the road and unpack his bundles and charge him well-nigh what he liked. If a man could not pay, sometimes the tax-collector would offer to lend him money at an exorbitant rate of interest and so get him further into his clutches. Robbers, murderers, tax-collectors were all classed together.[9]

A Jewish tax collector was so hated that he couldn't go into the synagogue. That's what they thought of him.

Because he could charge anybody whatever he wanted, the tax collectors were always rich. They never could get enough money. Jericho was a very wealthy area, and so it would be a fabulous place for a tax collector, and little Zacchaeus really raked in the money.

When some of the publicans went to John the Baptist and they asked, "What shall we do to repent," John the Baptist said, "Exhort no more than that which is appointed you. Don't charge any more than the Roman government appoints."

A tax collector was like the worst sinner anyone could imagine. It was the worst thing you can be.

To make matters worse, this chief publican lived in Jericho, and Jericho was like the Las Vegas of today. Much trade passed through Jericho. It was an artery from the East to the West for all Judean trade, and people also took their vacations there. The tax collectors of Jericho were not like the modern IRS, but more like the modern Mafia in how they took money.

So Jericho was the home of this miserable, thieving little guy named Zacchaeus. His name means "pure and innocent." Talk about somebody who let down his name! He was a thief, and a rogue, and an unscrupulous man, and someone who'd take the shirt off your back. That's what he was, Lord have mercy.

Zacchaeus heard that Jesus was coming through Jericho, and he wanted to see Jesus. Saint Luke says, "He sought to see Jesus, who he was." Jesus was about done with his whole ministry. He'd been healing and doing all his miracles, so he was known everywhere. Zacchaeus naturally wanted to see him.

By the way, one of the disciples of Jesus was a tax collector—Matthew sat at the receipt of customs, and so he was a tax collector who converted.

Clarence E. Macartney says,

> There is an old tradition, and a very beautiful one too, that when Matthew the publican was received into the band of the disciples, he said one day to Jesus, "Master, if you ever go through Jericho, I hope you'll look up an old friend of mine, the chief publican there named Zacchaeus."[10]

That might be true; I like to think it was. We'll find out when we get to heaven. Either way, Zacchaeus wanted to see Jesus.

Maybe it was just curiosity. Perhaps with all his wealth, Zacchaeus still wasn't happy and was searching. Perhaps he could see some of the poor widows that he had cheated out of money. He could see the little children tugging at their mother's skirts, while he was taking the bread out of their mouth. Maybe some conviction was coming to this little runt, this little rascal.

But being a short man, he couldn't see anybody in a crowd. And who was going to make way for a tax collector? They just elbowed him out of the way. So he shinnied up a sycamore tree, and there he was, and he could see what was happening. Pretty soon, here came the procession. They were coming down the road, and Jesus was coming, and Zacchaeus had a very special place, and they were going to go right under that sycamore tree, and Zacchaeus was really going to get to see him.

As they were going under that tree, they stopped. And we read that Jesus came to the place, looked up, and saw Zacchaeus, and said unto him, "Zacchaeus, make haste. Come down, for today I must abide in thy house."

The little man almost fell out of the tree. He was so thrilled that he would be able to see Jesus and talk to Jesus. So he took Jesus to his sumptuous home. They got behind closed doors, and they did some talking. Just what they said we don't know, but we know that the people didn't like it. They fussed, and they said, "He's eating with a sinner." They murmured. They complained. They fumed. They griped, and they grumped, and they gossiped.

They didn't like Jesus having any association with this sinner, but Jesus said, "I came to save sinners." He didn't come to save the righteous. He came to save the unrighteous. That's who he was interested in.

Behind these closed doors, we don't know what happened. But pretty soon, the doors opened, and Zacchaeus came out, and he was saying that he was going to be following the Lord, and that he was going to sell all that he had. He was going to give to the poor, and if he'd robbed anybody, he was going to give them fourfold over.

Jesus said, "This day is salvation come to this house." Now that doesn't mean that Zacchaeus was buying his way in; it means that he had been born again. It means that Zacchaeus, like Nicodemus, had accepted Jesus, and he was a changed man, and he was going to make restitution the best he could. Some time later, he came out and he told the whole crowd about all these things, because they hadn't gone home. They'd stayed there. They were still there, fussing around. And Zacchaeus said this wonderful thing. The little fellow wasn't done. He said that he was going to live for the Lord, because he was going to give all that he had, and he was going to serve Christ and follow Christ.

G. Campbell Morgan writes this about Zacchaeus:

> Something had taken place in that period of personal dealing between himself and Jesus. A radical change had taken place in the man. The habit of his life might have been expressed in the words "I get." He now is saying "I give." He had entered, mastered by greed. He came out, mastered by grace.[11]

What happened behind closed doors? We can only speculate, but Jesus talked to him maybe just like he talked to Nicodemus, and this man Zacchaeus—like Nicodemus—put his faith in Jesus, and was born again.

What does this story tell us?

Well, it tells us first of all that Jesus knows your name. That's something I want you to be sure to get.

Imagine Zacchaeus up in the tree, and the streets are packed with people. You can hardly walk. And Jesus comes and looks up at him and calls him by name. Of all these hundreds and thousands of people, he knows Zacchaeus. That almost made Zacchaeus fall out of the tree. Jesus looked up at Zacchaeus, and Zacchaeus must have felt like a treed raccoon up there. Only it wasn't a raccoon, but a dirty little thief. Then the unthinkable happened. Jesus said, "Zacchaeus, make haste. Come down.

Today, I'm going to abide in your house." Jesus knew his name.

Jesus knew Nathaniel's name before he met him. And Jesus knew Zacchaeus's name before he met him, and he knows your name, and he knows my name. He knows all about us, and he knows every sin we've ever committed. He knows every evil thought we've ever had. He knows all the good that we pass by and fail to do, and yet Jesus loves Zacchaeus, and he loves you, and he loves me, in spite of our sin.

When Jesus left Zacchaeus's house, he went on to Jerusalem, and at Jerusalem, he's going to die on a cross to pay for Zacchaeus's sins, and my sins, and your sins, and the sins of the whole world. That's what he did.

Jesus knows your name, and in this very moment, he may call your name. He may tell you to take him into your home. He may tell you that he wants to talk to you. He may call upon you to receive him. He may call on you to abandon some sinful ways. He may call on you to make up with somebody. He may call on you to give up some of these grudges that we carry.

He knows your name. Listen carefully. And then, like Zacchaeus, obey. That's what Zacchaeus did.

Then the second thing is, Jesus calls for action.

Jesus said, "Zacchaeus, make haste." If he'd tell me to make haste, I'd probably sit there petrified. But Zacchaeus made haste; he came down, and he received Jesus joyfully. Zacchaeus did not hesitate a second. He could have said, as I've had people say, "Oh, I'll wait till another time; I've got to think this over; this is a big step. I think I'll just wait until the crowd is gone. I'm just not quite ready yet." I don't know what Zacchaeus said or thought, but I know this. He answered the call immediately. And he went to work for the Lord.

Now, the devil is going to try to get you to put it off. He won't have you say, "No, I'll have nothing to do with Jesus." No, he's smarter than that. He just says, "Wait. Wait. Wait." *Wait…until you're into hell.* That's what Satan wants.

He doesn't want you to denounce Jesus. He doesn't want you to rail against Jesus. He just wants you to put it off.

This man Zacchaeus, if he had put it off, would never have found Christ. Because Jesus never went to Jericho again. After he left Jericho, he went to Jerusalem, where he went to the cross and the grave, and then his ascension. He was done, and this was the only time for Zacchaeus. Never again would Zacchaeus get that chance.

You better not pass up your opportunity now.

I'm going to tell you, friend, there comes a time when you get your last chance. I don't know when it is. You may have a hundred chances, I don't know. But there's going to come a time when, for the last time, you can either accept or refuse Jesus Christ. I look back over my ministry, and I can see some people that we preached to and talked to, and they came with open arms and shed tears of joy to receive Jesus Christ. They've gone on to serve him and follow him, and they're in heaven now. They have long gone home to heaven.

And I've seen many who say, "I've got to think more about this." Or they'll say, "Well, you have to be awfully good to be a Christian, so I want to clean up my life first. Then I'll be a Christian." Don't do that. Come just the way you are, because you'll never get cleaned up.

One old pastor put it like this: "Just come as you are. Jesus doesn't clean his fish till he catches them." So you just give yourself to Jesus. He'll help you clean up. You can't do it alone, and he'll help you, and he'll give you new life. Make haste. Listen to Jesus. Come down out of that tree. Come down off that perch. Come down from that pride, that self-satisfaction. Come out of that self-righteousness of yours. Forsake it. Come to Jesus.

This could be your only chance; this could be your last chance, right now.

Don't pass it by. Pray right now. Just talk to Jesus. That's all. Tell him your heart, and ask him in.

The next thing we learn from the story of Zacchaeus is that Jesus demands humility. Zacchaeus had to humble himself. He was a rich man, probably one of the richest men in Jericho, if not *the* richest. He was the chief of the publicans. Here he was, climbing up into that tree like a monkey. And here Jesus was telling this publican what to do. Nobody told a publican what to do.

Jesus said, "Get down off that tree, and get home, and I'm going to come and visit you." Zacchaeus humbled himself. He humbled himself when he climbed up into the tree in the first place. He humbled himself by coming down when Jesus said, "Come down." He humbled himself by making haste when Jesus said, "Make haste."

I'm sure there are some people—I have seen it in my ministry—who never come, because they're too proud. There is many a husband whose wife is a dedicated Christian who loves the Lord and prays for that man every day, but he's too proud to say he's a sinner, and too proud to say in front of his wife, "I was wrong." That's hard to say.

Zacchaeus had to humble himself. And what did Jesus say? "Blessed are the humble."

Maybe it's time for you to come down off your perch, to get down off your high horse, and get down on your knees. Do like Zacchaeus—because your eternal soul is in the balance. Don't be afraid of what people say. Maybe they'll make fun of you. Maybe, if you start going to church and serving the Lord, they'll say, "What happened to Joe? He used to be at our parties; he's not with us anymore." Or, "Why did he let us down? He turned sissy, or something?"

Well, if you think it's so sissy, then carry the Bible with your books to school sometime. It's not easy to be a Christian. It's hard, and that's the way we want it. We don't want the cheap and easy way.

It says in our story in Luke that "they all murmured" when they saw Jesus going to be a guest at the house of Zacchaeus. They talked about him.

When God calls you to do something, to preach something, to promote something, to stand for something, if God lays it upon your heart, never worry about what people say.

I remember a man named Ironside. He was a dear Christian man, he accepted Jesus, but he wouldn't tell anybody at school. He said, "I don't want to tell the boys, because they'll laugh at me." And his mother used to say, "Harry, just remember this. The boys can laugh you into hell, but they can't laugh you out." Don't worry about what people say. Stand up and say, "I'm a follower of Jesus Christ."

Then the last lesson from this story that I want to mention is that Jesus changes people. "Therefore, if any man be in Christ, he is a new creature: all things are passed away; behold, all things become new." There's a change in our life.

Now, there are some morally good people. They're not going to change a lot. If you're a poor person, a drunkard in the gutter, and you quit drinking, then people can see a great change. But if you're a morally good person— and there's nothing wrong with being morally upright and morally good— but you come to Jesus to save you from sins, then your attitude will change, and your goals will change, and your motives will change, and your lifestyle is going to be a little different. It's going to change.

Jesus always brings change into our life. It may not show. It may not be some great thing. But in our heart and our soul, there will be change. Like one man said, "I used to hate preachers. If I would see one coming down the street, I'd cross over to the other side. Now I have a preacher as my best friend." His attitude changed, and he had a heart for Jesus.

I've seen people who are struggling in sin, but they have a heart for Jesus.

Look at David. Look at what he did. Why, he committed adultery, and then to cover it up, he had a man killed. And yet God called David "a man after my own heart." What's he talking about? He's talking about David's heart, a heart that changes.

We need a change in our society. More laws? No. We need hearts that are changed. That's what it is.

When Jesus comes, he accepts you, and he helps you, and he makes it so that we can serve the Lord and follow the Lord.

Clarence Macartney says it so well. He says people sometimes hate to embrace Christianity and come into the church, lest it cost them something, or lest they give up this or that worldly pleasure. But when you have genuine repentance like that of Zacchaeus, it's not a question of, "What will I be required to give up," but rather, "What can I give to my Lord who sought me and found me and died for me?"

Zacchaeus was truly born again. And let me tell you two things. Don't forget. Giving his wealth didn't save his soul or make Zacchaeus a Christian. Don't get that wrong. Zacchaeus gave up his wealth because he became a Christian. The second thing is that rich people can be saved, as hard as it is. It's hard for those who have riches to enter the kingdom of

God; that's what Jesus said. But Jesus also said, "What is impossible with men is possible with God." It's better not to give up on anyone, because God seeks us, and God will save us.

Heavenly Father, we thank you for this beautiful story, because it tells about a man who really was an outlaw. He was a despicable man, and he hurt others, and he took money from widows who couldn't afford it, and he had no heart, and we would wonder if he had a soul. But he did have a soul, because everybody does. We're just so thankful that this man came to Jesus, and he was made whole, and he made restitution, and he goes down in the Bible as a man who loved you and trusted you.

We thank you, Lord, that you don't turn your back on anybody. "Him that cometh unto me, I will in no wise cast out"—this is what you promised, and that anybody can come, no matter how sinful they might be, no matter how grievous their sins might be. If they just come to you, you'll wash them. As Isaiah tells us, "Come now, let us reason together, saith the Lord; though your sins be as scarlet, they shall be as white as snow; though they be red like crimson, they shall be as wool." All because, as Saint John says, "The blood of Jesus Christ cleanseth us from all sin." So, Lord, today, may many come to you.

To those who are having hard times—maybe they lost a spouse, maybe they lost a child, maybe they lost a best friend, maybe they lost their job, maybe there's trouble in the home—O God, the devil afflicts all of us. He afflicts the Christians and the non-Christians alike, because that's his business. So help us to love you, to put our faith in you. May many do that today, and help all of us to rest on you.

In Jesus' name. Amen.

Jesus:
Our Great Sacrifice

15

Jesus:
Our Great Sacrifice

Luke 23:32-47

[32] And there were also two other, malefactors, led with him to be put to death.

[33] And when they were come to the place, which is called Calvary, there they crucified him, and the malefactors, one on the right hand, and the other on the left.

[34] Then said Jesus, Father, forgive them; for they know not what they do. And they parted his raiment, and cast lots.

[35] And the people stood beholding. And the rulers also with them derided him, saying, He saved others; let him save himself, if he be Christ, the chosen of God.

[36] And the soldiers also mocked him, coming to him, and offering him vinegar,

[37] And saying, If thou be the king of the Jews, save thyself.

[38] And a superscription also was written over him in letters of Greek, and Latin, and Hebrew, This Is the King of the Jews.

[39] And one of the malefactors which were hanged railed on him, saying, If thou be Christ, save thyself and us.

[40] But the other answering rebuked him, saying, Dost not thou fear God, seeing thou art in the same condemnation?

[41] And we indeed justly; for we receive the due reward of our deeds: but this man hath done nothing amiss.

⁴² And he said unto Jesus, Lord, remember me when thou comest into thy kingdom.

⁴³ And Jesus said unto him, Verily I say unto thee, Today shalt thou be with me in paradise.

⁴⁴ And it was about the sixth hour, and there was a darkness over all the earth until the ninth hour.

⁴⁵ And the sun was darkened, and the veil of the temple was rent in the midst.

⁴⁶ And when Jesus had cried with a loud voice, he said, Father, into thy hands I commend my spirit: and having said thus, he gave up the ghost.

⁴⁷ Now when the centurion saw what was done, he glorified God, saying, Certainly this was a righteous man.

WE'RE LOOKING NOW AT THE CRUCIFIXION OF JESUS, and of Easter Sunday as well. That Sunday is the high point of the Christian year, because we celebrate the resurrection of Jesus Christ from the dead. That's why the gospel is good news, and that's why I love to preach it.

Just a few days before he was crucified, Jesus rode into Jerusalem. He came from Bethany over the Mount of Olives. He came down the slope of the Mount of Olives. He crossed the little brook called the Brook Kedron, and he rode up the other slope into the holy city, Jerusalem.

He was coming as a king. Hosannas rang out from the multitudes along the way, and they cast down their garments, and they put down palm leaves along the way. They were crying out, "Hosanna, hosanna," which means, "Save now, save now." It's a quotation from Psalm 118:25-26, where we read, "Save now, I beseech thee, O LORD: O LORD, I beseech thee, send now prosperity. Blessed be he that cometh in the name of the LORD: we have blessed you out of the house of the LORD." So the triumphal entry took place.

But I'm going to tell you, friend, it didn't last very long. Because very soon they were going to condemn him to death. They were going to call for his death, and they were going to call for him to be killed—not by stoning, even though that was the Jewish way of doing it. They would call for him to be crucified. That is a most terrible, horrible way of dying that you can imagine. As a matter of fact, there's no place in the world today where crucifixion is practiced as capital punishment, even by the most barbarous of civilizations. It was a horrible way to die.

Saint Luke writes about the cross in Luke 23:33: "And when they were to come to the place which is called Calvary, there they crucified him, and the malefactors, one on the right hand and the other on the left."

I want to take just four words out of that verse for this sermon: "There they crucified him."

There they crucified him.

Jesus Christ was crucified within the environs of the so-called holy city. Somebody expressed it like this: "The holiest person who ever lived died the most unholy death ever experienced in the most holy place on earth."

So they took Jesus to the cross. *Calvary* is the Latin for the Greek *Golgotha*, which comes from Aramaic and Hebrew roots. Both words mean "the place of a skull." Jesus Christ was crucified on a hill that looked like a skull.

Now, what do you think about when you think of a skull? Well, for one thing, skull speaks of sin. A skull speaks of sin because had there been no sin in the world, there wouldn't be any skulls. Adam and Eve would have lived forever; there would have been no end to them if they hadn't sinned. But when they sinned, death came. This awful sin passed on to all people, and we're all sinners.

God describes his definition of our sins. It's in Romans 3, where Paul writes the mind of God and says,

> What then? are we better than they? No, in no wise: for we have before proved both Jews and Gentiles, that they are all under sin; as it is written, There is none righteous, no, not one: there is none that understandeth, there is none that seeketh after God. They are all gone out of the way, they are together become unprofitable; there is none that doeth good, no, not one. Their throat is an open sepulchre; with their tongues they have used deceit; the poison of asps is under their lips: whose mouth is full of cursing and bitterness: Their feet are swift to shed blood: Destruction and misery are in their ways: And the way of peace have they not known. (Romans 3:9-17)

And then Paul sums it up by telling them why these people live such a horrible life. He says, "There is no fear of God before their eyes" (3:18). They don't fear God, and they just live on in their sins. And so that place of a skull reminds us about sin, and how sin brought death to the human race.

The place of a skull also speaks of death. Death is the penalty of sin. Romans 5:12 says, "Therefore as by one man's sin entered into the world and death by sin, so death passed upon all men, for all have sinned."

Christ died in the place of death that he might become the victor over death, and so death for the Christian is not defeat. It is victory now, because Jesus Christ paid that price, and he beat death, and took the sting of death. When an unsaved person approaches death, they'll say to him,

"Prepare for the worst." And that's right. If you're an unsaved person, if you're an unbeliever, if you haven't received Jesus Christ, I'm going to tell you, that's exactly right. Prepare for the worst. But when a Christian dies, it is always for the best.

Saint Paul said in Philippians 1:21, "For me to live is Christ and to die is gain." And in 2 Corinthians 5:8, Paul says, "We are confident, I say, and willing rather to be absent from the body and present with the Lord." That's what we're aiming for; that's what we want.

Because of the death of Jesus Christ, we can say, as Paul said, "He hath abolished death." Through his death, we lose the fear of death. And so this mortal is going to put on immortality, and this corruptible is going to put on incorruption, because Jesus went to the place of a skull, and he died so that we might live. We are now the sons of God, the Bible says. We know not what we shall be until he comes, and then we are going to be like him.

A skull also speaks of corruption. Christ died on the cross, and you know that if somebody dies, pretty soon that body is going to go away. A skull speaks of this corruption. It speaks of how, in our own strength, we can't conquer death. But we can be like Job. Job said so clearly and plainly: "I know that my redeemer liveth, and that he shall stand in latter day upon this earth. And though, after my skin, worms destroy this body, yet in my flesh shall I see God, whom I shall see for myself, and mine eyes shall behold, and not another" (Job 19:25-27).

So we've got to have a victory over that death.

A skull also speaks about weakness. If a skull is left alone, it will go back to the dust from whence it came. There is no strength in it. No, it's a place of weakness.

When Jesus died on the cross, it looked like a place of weakness. It looked like Jesus Christ was a victim there, and he couldn't do anything about it. And they were taking his life. But it became the most powerful place in all the world, because Paul says, "God forbid that I should glory save in the cross of the Lord Jesus Christ." He says, "I'm not ashamed of the gospel of Christ. It's the power of God unto salvation."

That place of weakness became a place of power, because there he beat death and he beat Satan. It's a place of emptiness, and that skull is empty, the brain is gone, and it's an empty thing. That's a picture of people in the world. If you don't have Jesus Christ, you're empty, and you'll never be filled and never be full until you come to Jesus Christ. Because we're all made for God, and there's a place for us, a compartment for us. And we can have all the things of the world, but unless we have God in our life, we're never happy and we're never satisfied.

The place of a skull. "There they crucified him."

Who are "they"? Well, the Jews for one. Because the Jews laid hold of him in Gethsemane, and they took him to Annas and Caiaphas. They called for his crucifixion. They tried him in the Sanhedrin. They were the ones who said, "Crucify him, crucify him."

The Jews had a part, but the Romans had a part too. The Jews couldn't put anybody to death because they were under Roman rule. And that's why you have the crucifixion. Because that land was under Roman rule, and the Romans had capital punishment by crucifixion, while the Jews had it by stoning. But the Jews couldn't do anything on their own. That's why they took Jesus to Pilate. And what did Pilate say to him? "I have power to release thee. I have power to set thee free, and I have power to crucify you." The power was in Pilate's hands. He was a Roman.

So think of the Romans. They scourged him. They spit in his face. They put the purple robe upon him. They put the crown of thorns on his head. They mocked him and said, "Hail King of the Jews." That's the Romans.

The Romans laid the cross upon him. The Romans drove the nails through his hands. The Romans divided his clothing among them. The Romans cast their lots at the foot of the cross for the garment without seam. It was the Roman seal that was put on his tomb, and a Roman guard to keep him in the tomb. The Romans were there.

But I'm going to tell you something else, friend. You were there, and so was I. We were there because our sins put Jesus on the cross, and had we not been sinners, Jesus wouldn't have had to die. And so he went to that far-off country. All of us were lost in sin; he came into that country, and they didn't receive him. And what did they do? They cast him away. The hands of God exalted his Son; the hands of men crucified his Son; and you and I were in that far-off country.

I read the story of a man who had a dream one time, and he dreamed that he was there at the crucifixion of the Lord Jesus Christ. And a man came and he spat in the blessed face of Jesus. And then he saw that man take his fist, and he struck Jesus right square in the face. And then he took the crown of thorns, and he jammed those thorns onto his head. And this man who was dreaming said, "Stop." Then the attacker turned around, and it was himself. He was there.

> 'Twas I that shed the sacred blood,
> I nailed Him to the tree,
> I crucified the Christ of God,
> I joined the mockery.
> And of that shouting multitude
> I feel that I am one;

> And in that din of voices rude,
> I recognize my own.
> Around yon cross, the throng I see,
> Mocking the sufferer's groan,
> Yet still my voice it seems to be—
> As if I mocked alone.[12]

There's a famous picture by the artist Rembrandt entitled "The Three Crosses." When you look at that picture, the first thing you see is a cross with Jesus on it. Then you start to look around, and there's a mob of people with kind of ugly faces on them, and they're looking on as Jesus suffers. Then there's someone over in the shadows, another man looking on. Art critics say that that's a picture of Rembrandt. He put himself in that picture.

I'm going to tell you something, friend. You were there, and I was there. It wasn't just the Jews, and it wasn't just the Romans. It was our sins that put him on the cross. Somebody has put it like this:

> It's a simple thing to say that Christ died for the sins of the world. It's quite another thing to say that Christ died for my sins. It is a shocking thought that we can be as indifferent as Pilate, as scheming as Caiaphas, as callous as the soldiers, as ruthless as the mob, or as cowardly as the disciples. It wasn't just what they did. It was I who nailed him to the tree. I crucified the Christ of God. I join all that mockery.[13]

My friend, I'm going to tell you something. We were there standing in the shadows with Rembrandt, because we had a part in that.

When Jesus prayed, "Father forgive them, for they know not what they do," he was praying for you, and he was praying for me.

When Jesus Christ died on the cross, as I say, it's the most ignominious, the most shameful and horrible death that a person could be given, and no civilized country in the world uses crucifixion for capital punishment anymore. It was a death that was the most horrifying death you could know.

For instance, somebody put it like this:

> Bones would snap out of joint. The body was wracked with torture and thirst. His brow was pierced with the thorns. His back was lacerated from scourging. His hands and his feet were torn with nails. And that is why his visage was more marred than any man and his form more than the sons of men.

Isaiah writes about it. This is what he says in Isaiah 53:

> He is despised and rejected of men; a man of sorrows, and acquainted with grief: and we hid as it were our faces from him; he was despised, and we esteemed him not. Surely he hath borne our griefs, and carried our sorrows: yet we did esteem him stricken, smitten of God, and afflicted. But he was wounded for our transgressions, he was bruised for our iniquities: the chastisement of our peace was upon him; and with his stripes we are healed. All we like sheep have gone astray; we have turned every one to his own way; and the LORD hath laid on him the iniquity of us all. (Isaiah 53:3-6)

Isaiah goes on to say:

> He was oppressed, and he was afflicted, yet he opened not his mouth: he is brought as a lamb to the slaughter, and as a sheep before her shearers is dumb, so he openeth not his mouth. He was taken from prison and from judgment: and who shall declare his generation? for he was cut off out of the land of the living:

for the transgression of my people was he stricken. And he made his grave with the wicked, and with the rich in his death; because he had done no violence, neither was any deceit in his mouth. Yet it pleased the Lord to bruise him; he hath put him to grief: when thou shalt make his soul an offering for sin, he shall see his seed, he shall prolong his days, and the pleasure of the Lord shall prosper in his hand. He shall see of the travail of his soul, and shall be satisfied: by his knowledge shall my righteous servant justify many; for he shall bear their iniquities. Therefore will I divide him a portion with the great, and he shall divide the spoil with the strong; because he hath poured out his soul unto death: and he was numbered with the transgressors; and he bare the sin of many, and made intercession for the transgressors. (Isaiah 53:7-12)

That's the crucifixion, dear friend. That's what Jesus went through for us! He went through that for you and for me. Don't you see, when he asks us to receive him, and that's what we have done? He asks us maybe to suffer for him, or to witness for him, or maybe to give a tithe, ten percent, or maybe he'll ask like us, as he did with R. G Letourneau, "I need ninety percent of your income, Mr. Letourneau." And he gave it; he was faithful.

Maybe you'll have to go through hard times. But you will never go through anything as hard as Jesus went through. Long before you went through anything hard, Jesus had been there already, and he went to places that you'll never have to go. So let's not complain, but let's rejoice in such a wonderful, wonderful Jesus, who was crucified.

So somebody says, "If the Lord of glory had to die, why did he have to die in that way? Why did he have to die in such an ignominious death?"

Jesus had to do that. He had to do it because Old Testament prophecy said that he was going to be crucified. And if prophecy says it, if God says it's going to happen, it's going to happen. Just like the second coming of Christ; it's going to happen.

Psalm 22 is called the Psalm of the Cross. That psalm speaks about pierced hands and feet, and that's very peculiar. As I've said, the Jews stoned, they didn't crucify. Yet here in the Old Testament, David was saying that the Messiah was going to have his hands and his feet pierced, and it gives a graphic picture of the Lord Jesus Christ.

So the Lord of glory was sent to the cross because there was no other way for him to go.

Why was he sent to the cross? Prophecy said it, and then he had to go in order to save our soul. Look at him in the garden of Gethsemane. He knelt and he prayed, and he said, "Father, if thou be willing, remove this cup." That is, if there is some other way besides the cross, if we can do this any other way—let's do it.

He prayed, "If thou be willing, remove this cup from me. Nevertheless, not my will but thine be done." That's why we pray in Jesus' name, and we pray "Thy will be done." That's what he taught us to pray in the model prayer: "Thy will be done on earth as it is in heaven." That's what Jesus was praying. He prayed, "Not my will but thine be done."

It goes on to say. "And there appeared an angel unto him from heaven strengthening him." So God does that when we get into the hard times; he sends those angels. He'll send somebody to help you.

And then, being in agony, he prayed more earnestly. He sweat as it were great drops of blood falling down to the ground.

In Galatians 3, we read of two curses: "Cursed is every one that continueth not in all things which are written in the book of the law to do them" (3:10). That is, cursed is anybody that breaks the laws of God, the teachings of God. Then the second curse is in the thirteenth verse: "Cursed is everyone that hangeth on a tree."

Paul sums it all up, and he says, "Christ hath redeemed us from the curse of the law." We are not saved by keeping the law. Christ has redeemed us from that. We can be saved through grace and faith in Jesus Christ. And we try to keep the law, of course we do, but we can't help but break it. Then Paul says, "Cursed is everyone that hangeth on a tree." And that's why Jesus in his agony cried out on the cross, "My God, my God, why hast thou forsaken me?"

And I'm going to tell you, that was real. I heard a sermon one time, and they said, "You know, we all imagine things, and they're not as bad as they are, and God really hadn't forsaken his Son. Jesus just thought he had."

I'm going to tell you, that's not true to the Word of God. Jesus Christ knew that God turned his back on his Son. Because his Son, who the Father loved so much, carried our sins, the sins of the world. And God cannot countenance sin.

We do it all the time. We don't think anything about it. But God can't stand one speck of sin, and sin will never be in heaven.

Jesus is the Father's own Son, his only Son, the Son who the Father had never turned his back on in all eternity, nor ever will. But at Calvary, he turned his back on his Son, and it was such a horrendous thing that there was darkness over all the land, and an earthquake took place.

Why did he do it? He had our sins.

I'm going to tell you, we can crucify the Son of God yet today. In Hebrews 10, God is speaking to Christians, and he tells us that every unyielded believer, every one of us who knows what God wants us to do, and we don't do it, we trod underfoot the blood of Christ. He speaks of the "much sorer punishment" that is coming to anyone "who hath trodden under foot the Son of God, and hath counted the blood of the covenant, wherewith he was sanctified, an unholy thing, and hath done despite unto the Spirit of grace" (Hebrews 10:29).

And so what do we do? We put ourselves on the throne, and Christ on the cross, when it should be Christ on the throne and our lives on the cross. That's a message for Christians.

And so then they crucified him. Who was he? Really who was he? Well he was a man among men.

Paul says he was the Lord of glory, but he was a man among men. That is, he took upon himself the form of a servant, of a man; he was in the flesh just like you are. If God wanted Jesus to die on the cross, he could have created Jesus full-grown, just like he created Adam, and then have him go to the cross. But no, there's only one head of the human race, Adam.

When Jesus came, he came born of a virgin, born of a woman, and he grew to manhood, and as a man he went to the cross. He was a man among men. He took upon him not the nature of angels, but the seed of Abraham. And he went to the cross. "Wherefore in all things that behooved him to be made like unto his brethren, that he might be a merciful and faithful high priest in things pertaining to God, to make reconciliation for the sins of the people" (Hebrews 2:17). In other words, Jesus had to become one of us to save us. He had to go to the cross to save us. He could love us from heaven as God, but he could redeem us only by becoming one of us and dying for us.

He was a man above men. This wonderful Jesus. A man above men. That is, he was God incarnate. He was God and man, and there is nothing like that. There never will be another one just like Jesus Christ: Holy God and man combined into one.

And then, as a man for men, he became our sacrifice. So that we can come to Jesus Christ, put our faith and trust in him, and when we do, we'll find everlasting life. We'll find forgiveness, and we'll find peace.

I read the story of a young Scotsman named William Mackay, and he'd been brought up by a godly mother, and then he went to university as a medical student, and there he became an unbeliever. He rejected everything, and he became a member of the Hell's Club. And one time they were having a mock communion service. He held up the wine, and he said, "Behold the blood of the Lord Jesus Christ." He said that, and he began to tremble. Still trembling he ran out of that place, and he walked the streets of the city until almost morning. Then he went to his parents, he went back to his home, and he went to his room, and he wept. He said "I am guilty of the blood of Christ." And his mother heard him praying, and she went in and put her arms around him and prayed with him, and he accepted Jesus Christ.

He got up from that bed, and he stepped out of that room, and he went back to his people in the university to tell them what he had done. He said, "I accepted Jesus Christ as my Savior, and he's my Lord and my King." Not long afterward, he penned a hymn and the hymn begins like this: "We praise thee, O God, for the Son of Thy love, for Jesus who died and is now gone above."[14] He became a hymn writer and a minister of the gospel.

That's the reason Christ came. He came for men.

I want to ask you, dear friend, if you've accepted Jesus Christ. Maybe you're like William Mackay and you've drifted away, or you've never had the Lord, and you've made fun of the Lord, and you never listened to him, and now he's talking to you. What you need to do is tell him, "Dear God, I'm a terrible sinner, and I ask you to come into my life, dear Lord Jesus, and take away my sin. And I'll walk with you and I'll serve you the best I can all the days of my life."

You need to come to Christ, and maybe God is talking to you like he did to William Mackay, and you come and you respond. Come to Jesus, find everlasting life.

Dear heavenly Father, when we read this story, it makes us tremble as we think of the awful suffering Jesus endured, and that he did it for us. He had no sins. There wasn't a thing that would make him guilty. He said, "Can any of you charge me of sin? Let me hear it." But no one could charge him of a single sin. But he took our sins on himself on the cross, and that's where I should have been. That's where every sinner should have been, on that cross. But Jesus was there, suffering and dying for our sins.

So, dear heavenly Father, I pray that you'll speak to everyone who's reading this. I pray that you'll have your way in our heart and our life. Maybe we've drifted away from you. Maybe we've never accepted you. Maybe we do love you, Lord, but we're going through some hard times in life. Comfort our hearts and strengthen us, and help us to love you and submit to you entirely, so that your wonderful will might be done in our life and in our soul. Take complete control of our lives, and have your way.

In Jesus' name, amen.

Jesus: Our Coming King

Jesus:
Our Coming King
Matthew 24:32-44

[32] Now learn a parable of the fig tree; When his branch is yet tender, and putteth forth leaves, ye know that summer is nigh:

[33] So likewise ye, when ye shall see all these things, know that it is near, even at the doors.

[34] Verily I say unto you, This generation shall not pass, till all these things be fulfilled.

[35] Heaven and earth shall pass away, but my words shall not pass away.

[36] But of that day and hour knoweth no man, no, not the angels of heaven, but my Father only.

[37] But as the days of Noah were, so shall also the coming of the Son of man be.

[38] For as in the days that were before the flood they were eating and drinking, marrying and giving in marriage, until the day that Noah entered into the ark,

[39] And knew not until the flood came, and took them all away; so shall also the coming of the Son of man be.

[40] Then shall two be in the field; the one shall be taken, and the other left.

[41] Two women shall be grinding at the mill; the one shall be taken, and the other left.

⁴² Watch therefore: for ye know not what hour your Lord doth come.

⁴³ But know this, that if the good man of the house had known in what watch the thief would come, he would have watched, and would not have suffered his house to be broken up.

⁴⁴ Therefore be ye also ready: for in such an hour as ye think not the Son of man cometh.

WE'RE LOOKING NOW AT THE SECOND COMING of the Lord Jesus Christ. Jesus Christ came once, and he's going to come again. We know that because prophecy tells us.

In the Old Testament, the prophets of Israel prophesied to the whole world concerning Jesus Christ. Sometimes in their prophecies, the two comings of Jesus are put close together—the first and second comings. The prophets talked about when Jesus Christ is going to rule and reign over the whole earth. And that's the second coming. He didn't do that with the first coming.

We have New Testament promises. There are 260 chapters in the New Testament, and there are 318 references to the second coming of Jesus Christ. So in the New Testament, it's given over and over: Jesus is coming again.

Jesus himself said he would come again. He said in Matthew 26:64, "I say unto you, hereafter shall you see the Son of man sitting on the right hand of power, and coming in the clouds of heaven." Now that wasn't his first coming. He's coming again, this time in the clouds of heaven.

In Acts 1:11, the angels said that Jesus would come again: "Ye men of Galilee, why stand ye gazing up into heaven? This same Jesus, which is taken up from you into heaven, shall so come in like manner as ye have seen him go into heaven." This is when Jesus ascended into heaven, forty days after his resurrection. "This same Jesus" will return bodily, in his resurrection body—and not just in spirit. "This same Jesus, which is taken up from you"—that body that was taken up will come in the manner that those disciples saw him go into heaven.

There's no question about his second coming.

Paul talks about it in 1 Corinthians. James talks about it in the fourth chapter of his letter. Peter talks about it in his second letter. And John talks about in his first letter. Jesus is coming again.

Now, listen carefully, because when Jesus comes again, it's going to be in two phases. Two phases, or two aspects, or two parts, and they're called the rapture and the revelation.

The rapture takes place when Jesus takes all the believers, living and dead, catches them up in the sky, in the clouds, with him. That's the rapture.

The return and the revelation is when Jesus appears, and all the world sees him.

In the rapture, the rest of the world doesn't see Jesus. The Christians are just gone. But when the Lord comes, everyone is going to see him.

In the rapture, Jesus comes secretly to the church. He tells us in Matthew 24: "Two will be in the field, one shall be taken, the other left." They're just taken out. They vanish. And he says, "Two women shall be grinding at the mill." One will be taken, the other will be left.

And he says, "Watch, therefore, you know not the hour that your Lord will come." So that's the rapture. They're taken suddenly, and mysteriously they disappear.

But in the return, where Jesus is revealed, we read in Revelation 1:7,

"Behold, he cometh with clouds, and every eye shall behold him, and they also, which pierced him, and all the kindreds of the earth shall wail because of him."

All the world is going to see him. Now that's the revelation. With the rapture, no one sees him, but Christians are taken out. With the revelation, everybody sees him.

Let me tell you something. I started preaching in 1946. That's a long way down the road ago, and when I preached on how every eye shall behold him, and they also which pierced him, and some would say, "That's an error. The Bible has an error, because if Zechariah says he's going to have his feet on the Mount of Olives in Jerusalem, if he's in Jerusalem, how are you going to see him out here in South Dakota? Or Africa? Or wherever? It can't be."

We didn't have television. They didn't know anything about satellites or television, and all I could say is, "I don't know, but I'm going to preach it because God says it."

Well, now, you'll say, "Oh, they'll see us by television!" No, God's got something better than television. Because with television, they'll probably have technical problems. God's going to let the whole world see him.

So with the rapture, the Christians are taken out silently. With the revelation, the whole world sees him.

In 2 Thessalonians 4:17, Paul is talking to Christians, to believers, and he says, "Then we, which are alive and remain, shall be caught up together to meet them in the clouds, to meet the Lord in the air, and so shall we ever be with the Lord." We're to be snatched up. The dead are raised, and the dead in Christ are raised first. And then those of us who are alive will be taken up to be with the Lord. Read about it in 2 Thessalonians 4. It's all spelled out. That's silently, quickly; that's the rapture.

Now, the revelation we see in Matthew 24:30, where we read, "And then shall appear the sign of the Son of man in heaven: and then shall all the tribes of the earth mourn, and they shall see the Son of man coming in the clouds of heaven with power and great glory."

So you see, the return of Christ is in two parts: the rapture and the revelation. He'll come secretly for the church, and then openly for the whole world to see.

You'll see it again in 1 Thessalonians 4: "To meet the Lord in the air." That's the rapture. But in Zechariah 14:4, it says, "And his feet shall stand in that day upon the Mount of Olives, which is before Jerusalem on the east." So it tells us that he's coming back to earth, and it tells us the exact spot where he'll come!

And so, when we're caught up to meet the Lord in the air, that's the rapture. Then the revelation is when he comes and he stands on the Mount of Olives, just east of Jerusalem.

Here's one more I'll give you. Jesus says to Christians, "If I go and prepare a place for you, I will come again, and receive you unto myself, that where I am, there ye may be also" (John 14:3). So he's going to take us to be with him. No one else is going to see our departure; they're just going to notice that we're gone. All the Christians are gone.

And then, he comes for us: "I'll come and get you, and take you."

Then in 1 Thessalonians 3:13, Paul tells believers that he makes this request to God: "To the end he may stablish your hearts unblameable in holiness before God, even our Father, at the coming of our Lord Jesus Christ with all his saints."

So in the rapture, he takes us up, and then you have the tribulation, and some things that happen. And then Jesus comes again with the saints. So that's the second coming of Christ. It's the rapture, and then it's the revelation.

We have to be very careful we don't get these things mixed up, because some people say, "Well, it says one thing in one place, and says another thing in another place." Well, that's true, they are different. But he's talking about the rapture in one place, and he's talking about the revelation in another. So we need to be careful. As Paul says, we need to be "rightly dividing the word of truth."

And so, the Lord will come again. No question about it.

Now, with the second coming of the Lord Jesus Christ, he's going to be the sovereign Lord. He's going to rule and reign over all the earth, and Saint John describes it. He says,

> And I saw heaven opened, and behold a white horse; and he that sat upon him was called Faithful and True, and in righteousness he doth judge and make war. His eyes were as a flame of fire, and on his head were many crowns; and he had a name written, that no man knew, but he himself. And he was clothed with a vesture dipped in blood: and his name is called The Word of God. And the armies which were in heaven followed him upon white horses, clothed in fine linen, white and clean. And out of his mouth goeth a sharp sword, that with it he should smite the nations: and he shall rule them with a rod of iron: and he treadeth the winepress of the fierceness and wrath of Almighty God. And he hath on his vesture and on his thigh a name written, KING OF KINGS, AND LORD OF LORDS. (Revelation 19:11-16)

Jesus is coming again.

So the question is, are you going to be ready when Jesus comes again? Are you prepared for Jesus when he comes again?

Jesus talks about that in Matthew 24. He talks about the generation when he comes again as being like the generation of Noah, and he says, "They knew not, until the flood came and took them all away." He's talking about Noah's day. People weren't prepared. They had all kinds of warnings, but they weren't prepared. The flood came and took them away. And then Jesus says: "As it was, so shall it be." In other words, as it was in the days of Noah, so it's going to be in the days when Jesus comes again. Not a flood that will take people away, but the judgment of Almighty God is going to take them away. And they're not going to be ready. He says, "They knew not."

Why didn't they know? As Jesus compares the days of Noah and Lot with the days of the Son of Man, just study those days, and just look at them. Let's look at them for a minute. They say history repeats itself. And that's what it's going to do. They weren't ready for the flood, and at the return of Jesus Christ, people will not be ready for it.

The sin, the immorality, and the corruption and violence and godlessness of those days will be like the wickedness in the days of Noah. And so we have wickedness today, almost without measure. You take, for instance, the slaughter of the innocents, the horrible, horrible thing of taking the lives of these little children. Abortions by the millions! How wicked is that? How long is God going to wait until the judgment comes pouring on man?

But they never think of whatever happened, they went on with their work in Noah's day. They thought the sun would always shine, and there would always be another day. They expected the sun to always shine. And then it came: crash! God's wrath broke upon them, and they perished in the flood. They knew not. Why didn't they know? God warned them. Noah preached to them 120 years.

I've often thought about how I preach and I don't see anything happen, and I think, "Well, look at Noah. He preached 120 years, and didn't have a single person who responded rightly; nobody came forward, not a single convert." He had his family, but he preached his head off. And if you're a pastor who goes to a church wanting to preach, and you tell them, "Well, I haven't had a convert in 120 years," they'd say, "Move on, buster, you don't have it. I'm sorry. We don't need you."

Noah preached 120 years and had no results. Why didn't they know? He was building an ark! In other words, he lived what he preached. He built his ark in his cow pasture. It's a monstrosity of a thing. People didn't listen; they just went on with their lives. He preached, and he preached, and he warned, and he begged, but he had no takers.

Or look at Enoch. Enoch was a prophet in that day. And I was just saying the other day how there are only two people in this world who never died. Jesus? Not Jesus, Jesus died. But there are two people who were taken bodily into heaven: Elijah and Enoch. So Enoch is there, he's preaching. He's a godly man, and he walked with God, and one day God said, "You're closer to heaven than you are to the earth, come on in." And he took Enoch home. Physically, bodily.

Enoch was preaching, and what did he preach? Well, Jude tells us what he preached:

> And Enoch also, the seventh from Adam, prophesied of these, saying, Behold, the Lord cometh with ten thousands of his

saints, to execute judgment upon all, and to convince all that are ungodly among them of all their ungodly deeds which they have ungodly committed, and of all their hard speeches which ungodly sinners have spoken against him. (Jude 14-15)

So Enoch preached. They had a good preacher there.

I had a man tell me one time, "When you can preach a sermon like the Sermon on the Mount, I'll come to church." Well, is he crazy? How are you going to preach like Jesus preached? They'll use anything for an excuse. You don't want to go to church, so you can say you're eating soup with your knife. You can say anything. They don't want to come, they'll use any excuse. Just as they didn't listen to Enoch.

Then there was Methuselah. His name meant "when he is dead, it shall be sent." What would be sent? The year Methuselah died, the flood came. That's his name, everywhere he went, they were saying, "When he's gone, a judgment is coming. It's going to be sent." They didn't know about a flood, but they knew the judgment was coming.

Do you know who lived the longest in the whole Bible? That was Methuselah—he lived 969 years. That tells me that God kept giving people a chance, giving them a chance, giving them a chance. Because when Methuselah died, the flood was coming. God decided to let him live longer than any man in the whole Bible, to let people turn—but nobody turned.

Then they had something that sure ought to have shaken them to their boots. They had the filling of the ark, when from all over the country there came all these animals, and they came two by two and seven by seven. Why didn't they all come two by two? Because those that came seven by seven were the animals that were clean and that God would use for sacrifice. So he was providing these so that man could have something to give for a sacrifice. And that's why God has given you your talents and your money—he's given them for you to use for him.

But here came these two alligators, for instance. You'd be scared to death of them, thinking they were going to gobble you up. Nope, they headed for the ark. And skunks—you wouldn't want to get near those skunks. They were just as happy as they could be, and into the ark they went.

So, you know, that ought to turn something. Why didn't people listen? They didn't listen because they were like Demas, a young man mentioned in 2 Timothy 4:10, where Paul says that Demas forsook him, because he loved this present world. He loved this world. He wanted the things the world offered more than anything else. So he did not listen.

They knew not. Why didn't they know? Because they loved this world and they wouldn't listen to God.

If you're not a Christian today, why aren't you a Christian? Why don't you accept Jesus Christ? You want to live your own lifestyle. You don't want to repent. You don't want to turn. You want to stay in your sins. Well, when you accept Jesus Christ, you'll still have some sins, but you'll forsake the sins as best you can, and you'll turn from them.

I heard about a young girl who went to Dwight L. Moody and accepted the Lord. She asked Mr. Moody, "Now if I accept the Lord, will I have to give up my friends?" And Moody says, "No you won't have to give them up, they'll give you up. The minute you change your lifestyle, and you don't live like the hogs, but you live clean—they'll give you up."

Well, there are a lot of people who don't want to give up that old lifestyle. They'd rather go to hell with their friends. But there won't be any fellowship there! Hell will be solitary confinement. Forever and forever and forever, world without end. There won't be time anymore. Time started with the creation, and time is going to end with the new Jerusalem, and after that, there is no more time. It's just eternity. Forever eternal.

So you need to turn to the Lord.

They had their chances, but they only thought of earthly things. They were like Lot who settled in the Jordan Valley. Why did he settle in the Jordan Valley? Because Abraham said to Lot, "You choose whether you want the valley or you want this other part." The other part was practically wilderness. Lot chose the Jordan Valley, because it was well watered everywhere. He could have water and he could prosper, and he could get along. "But Abraham, you go on, you can have the desert out there, and wander around with your sheep and barely make a living. I'll take the world."

Why was it that they hated to leave Sodom and Gomorrah? Sodom and Gomorrah had been warned over and over again, and yet they stayed, they refused to move out, they refused to go. Poor Lot was saved by just the skin of his teeth.

The world has a way of getting hold of us. Money has a way of getting hold of us. You could have a million dollars, but if you don't know Jesus, that million dollars isn't worth a nickel. It isn't worth anything.

I read about one man who died, and he was a rich man. And a couple of the folks downtown were talking about him, and the one man says, "I wonder how much he left?" The other fellow said, "Well, I heard that he left everything." Yes he left it all, and lost his soul. That's the thing that we're up against today.

So we see this in Noah's day. They had a high civilization, and they had materialism and secularism. They had all kinds of sin and weakness, and you see it in the sins of Sodom and Gomorrah, the horrible sins of Sodom and Gomorrah. God hated it so much, he rained down fire and brimstone; today there's not a trace of those cities where they used to be.

We need to turn to God. We need to come to Jesus Christ. Then the question comes, a question they ask over and over: Yes, I know Jesus is coming again, but when? That's what the disciples said: "When will these things be? Dear Jesus, when are you coming again?"

So then we get into dates. But they've been asking that question for two thousand years. I've been preaching about sixty-five years. I know that at least three times, and probably more times than that, everybody got ready for the coming of the Lord: "The world is going to end, Jesus is coming." They put up billboards, and they put out publications and everything else. And they're just as crazy as a Dodo bird. Because nobody knows when he's coming again!

When you have somebody get up and they say that Jesus Christ is coming, he has his chart, and he has figured it all out. And he says, "Jesus Christ is coming at this certain time and this certain date." Either he doesn't know his Bible, or he's just as dumb as a Dodo bird. He doesn't know diddle.

Let Jesus answer. The disciples asked him that question. It's in Acts 1:6: "When they therefore would come together, they asked him, Wilt thou, at this time, restore again the kingdom of Israel?" That is, the Scriptures teach us in the Old Testament—Isaiah says it especially—that the government is going to be upon the Messiah's shoulders. He's going to rule on the throne of David, and he's going to rule the whole world, and that's what the Jewish people were looking for: the Messiah coming to rule over the whole world. And when he came the first time, they thought that was what he was going to do.

But when you study the Scriptures, they tell us that it's not going to happen until the second coming. So far it's been two thousand years since the first coming. We don't know how much longer it will be. And so people still say, "Will you at this time restore again the kingdom to Israel?" They're saying, "Jesus, are you going to come now?"

> And he said unto them, It is not for you to know the times or the seasons, which the Father hath put in his own power. But ye shall receive power, after that the Holy Ghost is come upon you: and ye shall be witnesses unto me both in Jerusalem, and in all Judaea, and in Samaria, and unto the uttermost part of the earth. (Acts 1:7-8)

Did you get that? "It is not for you to know the times or the seasons."

Remember this, my dear friend: *no one knows.* And God says, "I'm not going to tell you when Jesus is going to come, but I'm going to tell you something." What did he tell them? He says, "you're going to receive the power of the Holy Spirit, and I want you to be witnesses for me."

Jesus is saying, "Don't be getting out your pencil and doing your figuring."

I hear they even have books on this. And they're trying to figure out if this is the time when he's coming.

I don't know when he's coming. He could come before you're done with this chapter. We just don't know.

But I'm going to tell you something. If he waits, we're told in the Bible that a day with the Lord is a thousand years. If he waits for fifteen minutes, you got about a hundred years or so. So, don't get jumpy. Just do what Jesus says, and he says that he wants us to be his witnesses until he returns. "Forget about my return; forget about when I'm going to set up my kingdom. Just keep busy witnessing, telling others about my coming, about my salvation. That's your business! Your business is not to decipher or to calculate some time and try to out-guess God, or to pester God, so that you know about his coming. You know he's coming, that's all you need to know. Serve him. Follow him. Give to his cause."

You may have money; give it to those who are preaching the gospel. You may have more than you'll ever spend in this world. If you live longer than Methuselah, you couldn't spend it all. So give it to Jesus. Give it to the kingdom of God. See how many people can be won to Jesus.

That's the key, that's what it's all about. Witness for the Lord.

And another thing. *Take heart.*

Remember what Jesus said: "And when you see these things begin to come to pass, then look up. Lift up your heads, for your redemption draweth nigh" (Luke 21:28).

Are you discouraged today? Take heart. Are you without work? That must be hard; my heart goes out to you, and I pray for you, but take heart. There's a reason, a purpose for everything in life, and take any kind of job that comes along. Cleaning bathrooms or whatever it is—work.

And pray. We do pray that economic times will change, and you can get better work. Pray that for all of us. But just take heart, because Jesus Christ knows all about it. He's coming again.

Are you weary? Are you deep in sin? You think, "Oh, I knew the Lord, and I went into sin, and he's done with me. I blew it. He'll have no part with me." Read the story of Peter; he denied Jesus with cursing and bitterness. But when he came back, Jesus took him back. So take heart.

Esther Kerr Rusthoi has a beautiful poem that goes like this:

Oft times the day seems long, our trials hard to bear,

We're tempted to complain, to murmur and despair;

But Christ will soon appear to catch His Bride away,

All tears forever over in God's eternal day.

Sometimes the sky looks dark with not a ray of light,

We're tossed and driven on, no human help in sight;

But there is one in heav'n who knows our deepest care,

Let Jesus solve your problem—just go to Him in pray'r.

Life's day will soon be o'er, all storms forever past,

We'll cross the great divide, to glory, safe at last;

We'll share the joys of heav'n—a harp, a home, a crown,

The tempter will be banished, we'll lay our burden down.

It will be worth it all when we see Jesus,

Life's trials will seem so small when we see Christ;

One glimpse of His dear face all sorrow will erase,

So bravely run the race till we see Christ.[15]

Dear heavenly Father, thank you for the exciting news that your dear Son is coming again. He came the first time, born of the virgin two thousand years ago, but now we know that he's going to come again. He ascended into heaven forty days after his resurrection, and you've said he'll come again, and we know it to be true.

What can we take from this, Lord? Not just to settle our curiosity, but we need to live for you and serve you and tell others, because the time is going to come when people won't be able to come to you anymore. And so help us today, Lord, and may we glorify your name.

Speak to us, Lord, everything you want us to say, and the way you want it said. Bless your people and strengthen them today. And for those who don't know you, or who are still in their sins, may the light of the gospel shine into their hearts. And may this be the hour, this be the day, when they will open their heart to the Lord and let the sun shine in.

So this is your day; may you have complete control over every part of it. Thank you.

In Jesus's name, amen.

Notes

1 Numerous versions of this story are available at several websites on the Internet. The original source is unknown. Here is a link to a 1998 printing of the story in a newspaper in rural eastern Kentucky: *http://bit.ly/2YqVVsg*

2 Clarence E. Macartney was a prominent conservative Presbyterian pastor in the first half of the twentieth century, and the prolific author of about eighty published works. Several Macartney quotes are included in this book; their exact source locations from within Macartney's numerous works has not been fully determined.

3 J. Oswald Chambers, *Robust in Faith* (Chicago: Moody Press, 1965), 44.

4 Warren W. Wiersbe, *Be Mature: Growing Up in Christ* (NT Commentary: James) (Colorado Springs: David C. Cook, 1978), 157.

5 "Learning to Lean," lyrics and music by John Stallings (b. 1938), ©1977 by the Benson Company.

6 William Barclay, *The Gospel of Matthew*, revised ed. (Edinburgh: Saint Andrew Press, 2001), 57-58.

7 From Ironside's *Notes on Selected Books: Luke*, Luke 15; https://www.studylight.org/commentaries/isn/luke-15.html)

8 From Ironside's *Notes on Selected Books: Luke*, Luke 15; https://www.studylight.org/commentaries/isn/luke-15.html

9 William Barclay, *The Gospel of Luke*, revised ed. (Edinburgh: Saint Andrew Press, 2001), 77.

10 This same supposition about Matthew and Zacchaeus is offered in a quote by Methodist evangelist George Stuart in G. Campbell Morgan's The Great Physician: The Method of Jesus with Individuals (original ed.: Fleming H. Revell, 1937; reprint ed.: Eugene, Oregon: Wipf and Stock, 2010), in his chapter on Zacchaeus, 249-256.

[11] G. Campbell Morgan, *The Great Physician: The Method of Jesus with Individuals* (original ed.: Fleming H. Revell, 1937; reprint ed.: Eugene, Oregon: Wipf and Stock, 2010), 255.

[12] From the hymn "I See the Crowd in Pilate's Hall" by Scottish writer and pastor Horatius Bonar (1808-1889).

[13] M. R. DeHaan, *Bread for Each Day* (Grand Rapids: Zondervan, 1980), 12.

[14] From the hymn "Revive Us Again" by William P. Mackay (1839-1885).

[15] From the hymn "When We See Christ" by Esther Kerr Rusthoi (1909-1962), © 1941, renewed 1969 Singspiration; © Copyright 1941 by NewSpring (ASCAP) (admin. by Brentwood-Benson Composer Publishing, Inc.).

Made in the USA
Lexington, KY
16 September 2019